country inspirations

country
inspirations

a treasury of creative ideas, with timeless appeal

liz trigg • tessa evelegh • stewart & sally walton

HERMES
HOUSE

This edition is published Hermes House
an imprint of Anness Publishing Limited
Hermes House, 88–89 Blackfriars Road, London SE1 8HA
tel. 020 7401 2077; fax 020 7633 9499

Publisher: Joanna Lorenz
Project Editor: Lindsay Porter
Designer: Janet James
Photographer for Country Decorating: James Duncan
Stylist for Country Decorating: Tessa Evelegh
Photographer and Stylist for Country Crafts and
Flowers and Country Cooking: Michelle Garrett
Illustrator: Nadine Wickenden

Photographs on pp 6–9, 14, 15, 36, 37, 56 and 57
by Steve Tanner

Previously published as *Glorious Country*

1 3 5 7 9 10 8 6 4 2

NOTES

Standard spoon and cup measures are level.

Large eggs are used unless otherwise stated.

Contents

Country Style

Picture a house in the countryside on a bright autumn day, smoke wafting from the chimney into a brilliant blue sky. There are trees that have turned glorious shades of yellow and orange and there is a chill in the wind. Cats are asleep in shafts of sunlight, ignoring the birds that chatter on the rooftop. On a summer day, the arch over the gate will be covered with roses, and hollyhocks will stretch up the white walls past the open windows from which curtains billow out, caught by the warm breeze. &. Step inside the house and smell bread baking in the range; leave your shoes on the rack and walk across the cool flagstones. Sink into a comfortable chair by the scrubbed pine table and look around at stenciled patterns, crocheted lace, gleaming copper pans and wooden spoons. This is the country that we see in our dreams, and if our waking hours are passed in a high-speed, high-pressure city environment, these dreams have an added seductive quality. Rosy images of the pastoral are potent symbols of a way of life that seems somehow gentler, less stressful and more natural than the urban routine. As the pressures of late twentieth-century living mount, we want to put some of that country tranquility back into our lives. One of the easiest ways of doing this is to recreate some elements of country style in the home, providing a restful and welcoming environment to come back to. You don't have to live in the country to create the country look: the look comes as much from a way of thinking as from a way of living. &. This book shows you how to get into that way of thinking, and how to create projects that will bring something of the dream of country living into your home — whether that is a farmhouse or an apartment. But it's not just the end product of your creativity that you will value; in the process of designing and making country-style artefacts and effects you will find a satisfaction and sense of peace that are the real goals of country style.

BELOW: *The beautiful yet practical nature of patchwork is typical of country style.*

Achieving a Country Look

Country style has many interpretations and all over the world there are city dwellers who dream of a calmer way of life in a place where traffic doesn't bustle, food has more flavor and night skies are filled with stars, not neon. This may be an idealized picture, but it has an underlying truth: country life is still governed by seasonal changes, not manmade deadlines. 🖤 Country homes are alive, growing and comfortable and country decorating is for living in, not just looking at. Many of the effects that we think of as talismans of country style have an eminently practical function. 🖤 Country style may vary a

lot, according to nationality and the local climate, but there is a core of recognizable elements. It is a home-made, functional, comfortable style. There is often a big kitchen area, with a large scrubbed pine table and an assortment of comfortable chairs. Country kitchens can be a riot of pattern and color, where the shelves are stacked with displays of china and the beams are hung with baskets full of drying flowers and herbs. Gleaming copper pots and pans should never be

hidden away in cupboards, so use butcher's hooks to display them out of "head banging" reach. Floors need to be practical, tough and easy to keep clean, so floorboards, flagstones, linoleum or cork tiles are the favorite choices, and they can all be softened with washable cotton dhurries or rag rugs. 🖤 The food prepared in the country kitchen is hearty and nourishing, and is prepared from the produce of the season — warming roasts and stews in the winter and light, fresh vegetable dishes or fruit pies in the summer. Locally grown produce — organic, if not from your own garden — will taste immeasurably

ABOVE: *Although several motifs are present in this room, the restricted use of color pulls the whole look together.*

better if it is a seasonal treat rather than a year-round staple. 🐦 Through-out the home, flower arrangements take their cue from nature and are combined with other organic materials to provide a more casual, spontaneous look than hot-house blooms. A vase that has been in the family for years stands alongside an enamel jug filled with flowers from yesterday's walk. You might choose to float flowerheads on a glass plate, or collect supple twigs to form a heart-shaped wreath wrapped with trailing ivy. The colors of autumn may be represented by gourds, vegetables and dried seedheads. 🐦 The country house is not a fashion statement, and its colour schemes should reflect the natural color in the landscape; these need not be dull, bland and safe; they can be as rich as autumn, with touches of brilliance, or warm as a summer pasture filled with buttercups or a field of ripe corn. 🐦 The house responds to personal touches; a painted border may still be there in 50 years, so paint it thoughtfully. Make time in your life to be creative, whether it is with stenciling, floor painting or embroidery. All homemade crafts add richness to the home and give you a sense of personal achievement that money cannot buy. 🐦 There are step-by-step projects here to suit all levels of experience and creative ability. You may feel daunted by embroidery but more confident about making patterns in tin with a hammer and nail; unsure about flower arranging, but able to place a few dried flowerheads into a terracotta pot.

BELOW: Decorative panels can transform a piece of furniture. If you are not confident about painting free-hand, stenciling is a simpler option.

Whatever you choose, rest assured that all the projects have been designed to give maximum effect for minimum effort. If you want a change of scene on your walls, use a color glaze with a foam-block print or stenciled border. Giving floorboards the limed look requires the hard work of sanding first, but the painting can be done and dried

ABOVE: *Patchwork cushions soften a wooden chair, and provide a practical use for odd scraps and remnants of fabric.*

in an afternoon. If you have considered laying cork tiles, then stain half of them black and make a real impact with a checker-board floor. ᘒ When it comes to choosing materials, or pieces of furniture to decorate, take a tip from the squirrel and start hoarding! There are so many second-hand stores, flea markets and yard sales, and if you buy things that have potential, you will always have something to hand when the creative mood strikes. It can be amazingly difficult to find a wooden tray or a nice tin can when you want one, so have a "potential" corner in the loft or the shed, and keep it well stocked! ᘒ On a very practical note, there has been a major change in materials for home-decorating recently, with the arrival of water-based paint products. There is no longer any need for solvents to clean brushes; they rinse out under the faucet. The biggest bonus of this revolution is that decorating time has been cut in half. Water-based products dry very quickly, and this is especially useful when applying many coats of varnish to painted furniture. The rule to remember is not to mix oil and water, so if you tint varnish for an antique effect, mix acrylics with water-based clear varnish or oil color with traditional varnish. ᘒ Whether you go for the total country look for your home, or just a few details, always try to decorate in a way that is sympathetic to the character and age of your house. Use the best features, like an interestingly shaped window, as focal points; be courageous about removing a ghastly fireplace, or disguising oppressively heavy beams. Your home should please you, and country style is about personal touches, natural materials, warmth and comfort. So, follow your instincts and enjoy the charm of country life.

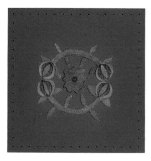

COUNTRY
Decorating

STEWART AND SALLY WALTON

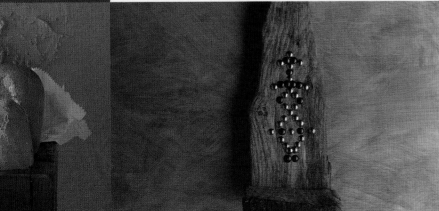

Walls and Floors

A coat of paint or an interesting floor covering will
transform any room, and will set the scene
for the total country look. Transform your walls
with stencils or a hand-painted frieze;
foam-block stamps look as authentic as hand-blocked
wallpaper, and are a fraction of the cost.
For floors, try limed-look floorboards, cork tiles,
or a trompe-l'oeil dhurrie.

The Country Palette

Color has a great influence on us: it can affect our moods quite dramatically. Choose your palette from nature's harmonies, avoiding artificially brilliant colors. It would be a mistake to think that natural colors are all shades of beige; just think of autumn and the huge variety of yellows, oranges and scarlets that mingle among the trees.

When painting the walls country-style it is best to avoid a perfect, even finish – go instead for a patchy, glowing, color-washed effect. By doing this you can use strong color, but in a transparent way that is not as heavy as solid color. Don't avoid strong colors, like brick red, deep green or dusky blue. The furniture, rugs, pictures, ornaments, cushions and curtains will all combine to absorb the strength of the wall color and dilute its power. If your rooms are dark, use the strong colors below chair-rail height only, with a creamy, light color on the upper walls and ceiling. Darker colors can be very cosy in a large room, but if you want a room to look bigger it would be best to stick to a lighter scheme, and use a stencil or freehand border to add color and interest.

If mixing your own paint is too daunting a prospect, you could go for one of the new "historic" ranges made by specialist producers. These paints are a lot more expensive than ordinary brands, but the color ranges are designed to harmonize with antiques, natural building materials and old textiles, and if your budget can stretch to them, they are really wonderful.

If your courage fails and you choose white walls, think about highlighting the woodwork. Paint a deep, rich color on the baseboards and the window- and door-frames, allow it to dry and then

ABOVE: *Colors derived from nature are not necessarily somber. Think of clear blue skies or a field of wildflowers.*

paint a light color on top. Use a damp cloth to wipe off some of the topcoat, and sandpaper to lift color that has dried. This will give you an effect of flashes of brilliance to add warmth to the room.

Choose natural colors that make you happy, and remember that country-style decorating is not about having everything matching. You don't need coordinating curtains, carpets and lampshades. On the contrary, the more eclectic the choice, the more stunning the effect can often be.

Giving your home the country look requires attention to the basics – the walls and floors. Get these right and the rest is easy. A bare room with powdery wall-paint, stenciling and a stripped, limed floor has a real country feeling, whereas no amount of folk artefacts and rustic furniture can transform to "country" a tastefully wallpapered, corniced and thick-pile carpeted drawing room!

The ideal way to begin would be to clear the house, remove all the old wallpaper

and carpets and start from scratch, but this is a luxury that few can afford. It's more practical to think in terms of a room at a time, repainting the walls and adding one of the country-style floors that are featured in this chapter.

This chapter shows how the basic elements of a room can be changed to make it feel more individual. When you paint, stencil or print on your walls, they truly become your own, and this never happens with wallpaper, however good you are at hanging it! We sometimes suggest cheating a little: roughening up smooth surfaces, wiping off more paint than is put on, or stenciling unevenly, for a worn-away look. You can't wait a hundred years for this to occur naturally!

The ideas for the projects have been inspired by folk art and by real-life examples of country decorating of period homes. There has been a recent revival of interest in the subject and it is now possible to buy kits to age practically anything, with a plethora of equipment required for the job.

Whatever you choose for your walls and floor, it is important to see them in terms of a backdrop for your own tastes and possessions. Paintings, mirrors, lamps, plants, shelves, rugs and furniture will all add to the final effect. A painted border may appear to be too dominant in an empty room, but the effect will be much more subtle when the furnishings, accessories and personal details have been added.

Remember that country style is more about relaxation, comfort and harmony than precision and fashion; this is the type of decorating that is a pleasure to involve yourself in, so enjoy the process as well as the result.

CLOCKWISE FROM TOP LEFT: *The walls and floors have been coated with tinted varnish to simulate the patina of age. Deep, brick red is bold, yet warm in a living room. The soft colors of this crazy patchwork quilt are punctuated with vibrant stitching.*

Brushed-out Color Glaze

This soft, patchy wall finish is pure country. It is traditionally achieved using either a very runny color-wash, or an oil-based glaze tinted with oil color, over eggshell paint. This project gives the same effect, but is easier to do.

The unusual element in the glaze is wallpaper paste, which is mixed in the usual way before the addition of white glue. The wallpaper paste adds a translucency to the color and the glue seals the surface when dry. To tint the glaze you can use powder, gouache or acrylic paint, mixed with a small amount of water first, so that it blends easily.

Use a large decorator's brush to apply the glaze, dabbing glaze on to the wall about five times within an arm's reach. Then use light, random strokes to sweep the glaze across the area, to use up the dabs and cover the area. Move along the wall, blending each area with the next.

This is a very cheap way of painting a room, so you can afford to mix up more glaze than you will use, and throw some away if there is some left over. This is preferable to running out before you finish, because it is so difficult to match the original color. 1¾ pints of glaze will cover almost 40 square yards.

MATERIALS

white glue
wallpaper paste
acrylic, gouache or powder paint,
to color the glaze
large decorator's brush

1

Prepare your wall-surface: ideally it should be an off-white satin, but any plain, light color will do, if it is clean. Wash old paint with wall cleaner and leave it to dry.
Mix up the glaze, using 1 part white glue, 5 parts water and ¼ part wallpaper paste. Tint it with three 8 in squirts from an acrylic or gouache tube, or about 1 tbsp of powder paint. Vary the intensity of color to your own taste. Experiment on scrap shelf liner painted with the same background color as your walls. Get the feel of the glaze and brush, and adjust the color at this stage if necessary.

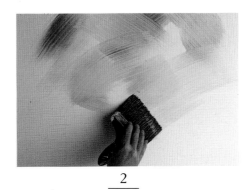

2

Begin applying the glaze in an area of the room that will be hidden by furniture or pictures; as your technique improves you will be painting the more obvious areas. Start near the top of the wall, dabbing glaze on with the brush and then sweeping it over the surface with random strokes, as described previously.

3

The effect is streaky and the brushstrokes do show, but they can be softened before they are completely dry. After about 5 minutes brush the surface lightly with your brush but don't use any glaze. The brush will pick up any surplus glaze on the surface and leave a softer, less streaky effect. When working on edges and corners, apply the glaze and then brush it away from the corner or edge. You will still find that the color may be more concentrated in some places, but it will all look very different when the room is furnished.

"Powdery" Paint Finish for Walls

You may need to rough-up your walls a bit to achieve this look; this is easily done with a tub of spackle, a spatula and some coarse-grade sandpaper. Think of it as the opposite of the usual preparations!

This paint finish imitates the opaque, soft color and powdery bloom of distemper, the wall finish most commonly used before the invention of latex paint. The joy of decorating with this "powdery finish" paint, is that it can be used directly on concrete, plaster or dry wall – indeed almost any surface – without lining paper or special undercoats. The paint is diluted with water to the consistency required, and is slapped on with a large brush. Mistakes and runs can be wiped off with a damp cloth, and the paint is a pleasure to use. It takes about two hours to dry, and the color lightens considerably as it does so, until the final effect is revealed – a soft powdery surface of matt color that will bring instant warmth to any room.

The "distressed" plaster effect has a charmingly country feel. Real country dwellers probably didn't have the time or inclination to decorate to a perfect finish; for whatever reasons, there is something very comfortable about walls with irregular surfaces and faded paint.

MATERIALS

spackle
spatula
coarse-grade sandpaper
latex paint in warm cream
large decorator's brush

1

Prepare the walls by stripping off any wallpaper down to the bare plaster. Spread the spackle irregularly with the spatula to simulate the uneven texture of old plaster. Use thin layers, applied randomly from different directions. Don't worry about overdoing the effect; you can always rub it down with sandpaper when it's dry, after about an hour.

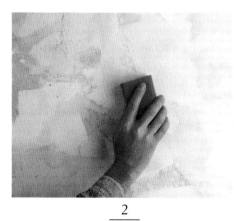

2

Blend the dried spackle into the original wall surface using the sandpaper, leaving rougher areas for a more obvious distressed effect. Mix the paint with water in the ratio 2 parts water to 1 part paint.

3

Begin painting at ceiling height. The paint is likely to splash a bit, so protect any surfaces with an old sheet or drop cloth. Use the paintbrush in a random way, rather than in straight lines, and expect a patchy effect – it will fade as the paint dries. The second coat needs to be heavier, so use less water in the mixture. Stir the paint well; it should have the consistency of light cream. Apply the second coat in the same way, working the brush into any cracks or rough plaster areas. Two hours later the "bloom" of the powdery finish will have appeared. The element of surprise makes decorating with this paint exciting, especially as the final texture is so mellow and effective at covering, but not concealing, the irregularities of the wall's surface. We used this surface as a base for the stenciled border on the following page.

Stenciled Border

Stenciling tends to spread around the house like a climbing plant, appearing round doorways and winding along picture rails, up staircases and across floors! It is a delightful and habit-forming activity, and it's extremely difficult to be a minimalist when it comes to stenciling.

The design used for this border came from a Rhode Island house that was built and decorated in the eighteenth century. Stenciling was an extremely popular means of decorating interiors, and stencils were used to create pillars and friezes as well as allover patterns, with as many as seven different designs on a single wall.

A border design like this one is perfectly suited for use above a chair-rail, but there is no reason why you should not use it at picture-rail, or baseboard height, or even as a frame around a window. Or you may not have a chair-rail but still like the

effect of a wall divided in this way. In this case it is a simple matter of marking the division with paint or varnish.

Use a plumb line and a long ruler to divide the wall, marking the line in pencil. The wall below the line can be painted a darker shade, or, if you are using a warm cream color, a coat of clear satin varnish will darken the color and add a sheen. The stenciled border will visually integrate the two sections of wall and soften the edges between them. If you vary the depth of stenciled color, it will look naturally faded by time.

MATERIALS

tracing paper
Mylar or stencil cardboard
spray adhesive
craft knife
masking tape
latex paint in
warm cream (optional)
varnish in shade "Antique Pine"
household paintbrush
stencil paint
stencil brush

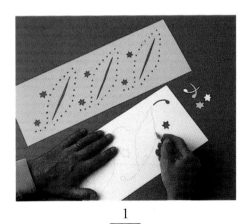

1

Trace and enlarge the pattern from the template section. Stick it on the Mylar using spray adhesive. Use a craft knife to cut out the stencil carefully. Repair any mistakes with masking tape and always use a very sharp blade which will give you the most control when cutting. Peel off the remaining tracing paper.

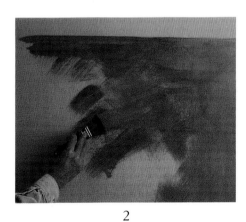

2

If desired, prepare the powdery paint finish on the previous page, then paint the whole wall in warm cream. Paint the lower half of the wall with a coat of Antique Pine tinted varnish. Use random brush strokes for a rough finish.

W A L L S   A N D   F L O O R S

3

Apply a light spray of adhesive to the back of
the stencil and leave it to dry for 5 minutes.
Position the stencil at a corner and paint the
first color. Use the paint very sparingly,
wiping the brush on absorbent paper towels
before using it on the wall. You can always
go over a light area to darken it later, but
excess paint on the brush will cause blobs,
and bleed through to the back of the stencil.
Lift the stencil and wipe any excess paint
from the pattern edges before positioning it
alongside the stenciling. Continue along
the top of the chair-rail until the first color is
complete.

4

Stencil paint is fast-drying, so you can
immediately begin to add the next color,
starting at the same point as you did with the
first. Work your way around the border,
remembering to wipe the stencil clean
as you go.

Freehand Frieze with Semi-gloss to Chair-rail Height

*This project combines the idea of dividing up the wall with textures and colors,
and the freehand painting of a vine frieze. The frieze will take some planning
and preparation to achieve the casual freehand effect, but the finished painting
will look effortless and be unique.*

A coat of gloss paint below the chair-rail will provide a practical, tough, wipe-clean surface where you most need it, and the gloss gives the color a marvelous reflective shine. The lighter color above the dado has a matt texture and the shade is reminiscent of cream straight from the dairy. If you don't have a chair-rail dividing your wall, this project is just as effective on a plain wall.

The secret of painting freehand curves on a vertical surface, is to steady your hand on a maulstick, which is quite simply a piece of dowelling about 18 in long. Make a small pad of cotton wool at one end, cover it with a small square of cotton or cheesecloth and secure it with a rubber band. Use the stick by pressing the pad against the wall with your spare hand, holding the stick free of the wall. Rest your brush hand lightly on it to prevent wobbles and jerks. Practise the curves with the maulstick before starting the frieze, but remember that the charm of hand-painting is its variability, so relax and enjoy yourself.

MATERIALS

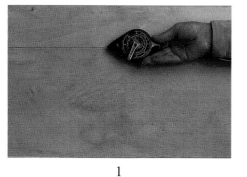

latex paint in deep yellow
full gloss paint in deep blue
oil eggshell paint in brick red
paint-roller and tray
fine nap roller
1 in decorator's brush
masking tape,
if necessary
chalk line or ruler
chalk
tracing paper
stencil

scalpel or craft knife
½ in square-ended artist's
brush
gouache paint in Indian red and
raw sienna
18 in length of dowelling
(of pencil thickness)
small wad of cotton wool
square of cotton fabric
rubber band
number 6 round-ended artist's
brush

1

Apply yellow latex to the prepared wall with the paint-roller, from ceiling to chair rail. Paint blue gloss color between the chair rail and baseboard, using the fine nap roller. Using the red eggshell paint, and the 1 in brush, paint the baseboard and the chair rail, if you have one. Use masking tape, if necessary, to give a clean line. Use a chalk line or ruler to draw light chalk guidelines, marking out the depth of the frieze.

2

Using your chosen stencil, lightly mark out the position of the frieze by drawing through the stencil.

3

Paint the thick and thin lines, using the square-ended brush, flat and on its side, and the gouache paints. To add variety to the line, mix up two different shades of the same color and use both randomly.

4

Make up your maulstick as described on the previous page.

5

Paint in the curved stems, using the round-ended brush and gouache, supporting your hand on the maulstick. Try to make your movements as fluid as possible.

6

Add the bunches of grapes, above and below the stems using the round-ended brush. Overlap the double lines in some places: remember that you are aiming for a hand-painted look, not a regular-repeat pattern.

Foam-block Painting

Printing with cut-out foam blocks must be the easiest possible way to achieve the effect of hand-blocked wallpaper, and it gives an irregularity of pattern that is impossible in machine-made papers. Another special feature of this project is the paint that we have used – a combination of wallpaper paste, white glue and gouache color. This is not only cheap, but it also has a wonderful translucent quality all of its own. The combination of sponge and paint works well, because pressing and lifting the sponge emphasizes the texture that results from using a slightly sticky paint.

The best foam for cutting is high in density but still soft, such as upholsterer's foam; it needs to be at least 1 in thick. You need to be able to hold the foam firmly without distorting the printing surface.

Paint some of your background color on to sheets of scrap paper, and then use this to try out your sponge-printing; use different densities and combinations of color, making a note of the proportions of color to paste in each one. This means

you will be able to mix up the same color in a larger amount when you print on the wall (although the paint will go a very long way). The background used here is painted using the brushed-out color glaze described on page 16.

MATERIALS

tracing paper, if necessary
upholsterer's foam scraps
felt-tipped pen
craft knife
plumbline
paper square measuring 6 × 6 in,
or according to your
chosen spacing
wallpaper paste
white glue
gouache paint or ready-mixed
watercolor paint in viridian,
deep green and off-white
saucer
clear matt varnish (optional)

1

Photocopy or trace the design from the template section and cut out the shapes to leave a stencil. Trace the design on to the foam and outline it using a felt-tipped pen.

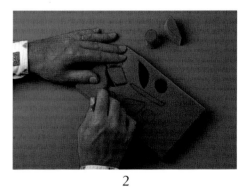

2

Cut out the shapes using a sharp craft knife: first cut around the pattern, and then part the foam slightly and cut through the entire thickness.

3

Attach the plumbline to the wall/ceiling join in one corner. Now turn the square sheet of paper on the diagonal and let the plumbline fall through the center, lining up the top and bottom corners with the line. Make pencil dots on the wall at each corner. Move the square down the line, marking the corner points each time. Then move the line along sideways. Continue until the whole wall is marked with a grid of dots.

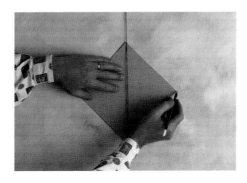

4

Mix wallpaper paste and water according to the manufacturer's instructions. Add white glue, in the proportion 3 parts paste to 1 part glue. Add a squeeze of viridian and deep green gouache paint or ready-mixed watercolor, and blend the ingredients until well mixed. Test the mixture on scrap paper, adding more color if necessary.

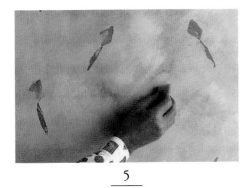

5

Put some paint into a saucer and dip the first sponge into it. Wipe off excess paint, and then print with the sponge using a light rolling motion. Lift and print again, using the pencil dots as a positioning guide.

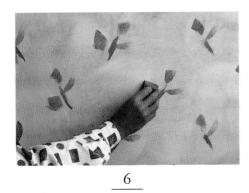

6

Use the second sponge to complete the sprig design with leaf shapes, varying the position slightly to add life.

7

Use the dot-shaped sponge and the off-white color to complete the motif with berries, adding the color to the glue mixture as before. Go over the leaves or stalks on some sprigs and let others "float" alongside. If your walls are to be exposed to steam or splashes, or even fingerprints, you may want to protect this finish with a coat of clear matt varnish.

"Limed" Floorboards

Liming sanded wooden floorboards gives a much softer impression than stains or tinted varnishes, reminiscent of scrubbed pine kitchen tables, washed-out wooden spoons, or driftwood bleached by the sun and the sea. If you are lucky enough to possess a sandable floor, try this easy alternative to time-consuming conventional liming. The floor can be a traditional off-white, or tinted to any pastel shade.

Raising the grain in the wood with a wire brush makes the channels for the paint, as well as clearing out any residual polish or varnish. If you like the wood grain to show as much as possible, wipe the surface with a damp cloth before it dries; the color will then be concentrated in the raised grain of the floorboards. When the floor is dry, a coat of acrylic floor varnish will seal the color.

MATERIALS

coarse wire brush
white latex paint
acrylic paint in raw umber
large decorator's brush
clean damp cloth
clear matt varnish

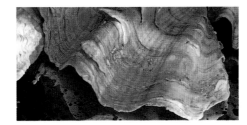

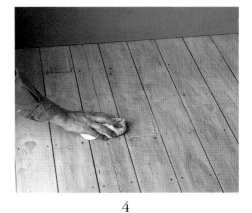

1

Use a wire brush to raise the grain in the wood following the grain direction at all times. Brush and vacuum the floor carefully.

2

Mix up the wash, using 3 parts of water to 1 part of latex. Tint the color with raw umber acrylic, or, if you prefer, use a pastel color: pink, blue, green or yellow will all look good in the right setting, and very little of the actual color will show. Experiment on spare boards.

3

Apply the wash with the decorator's brush, beginning in a corner at the baseboard and following the direction of the grain to the other edge.

4

Use a damp cloth to wipe away any excess paint and reveal the grain. A wet cloth will just wash away the paint, so keep it just damp for this. When the floor is completely dry, apply several coats of varnish to protect and seal the surface, allowing plenty of drying time between each coat.

Masonite Floor with Trompe-l'œil Dhurrie

It is a sad fact that not every home is blessed with handsome floorboards, to be sanded and waxed to a golden gleam. Most older houses have a mixture of new and old boards that aren't good enough to be made into a feature.

Masonite can be a surprisingly attractive solution if you're faced with a low budget and a patchy selection of floorboards. The utilitarian appearance of masonite means it is most often used as a leveling surface below linoleum; used in its own right, however, and decorated with stencils, it can look very stylish.

To counteract the potential drabness of a large area of masonite this project shows how to paint a trompe-l'œil dhurrie in the center of the room, so that the plain board becomes the border for the dhurrie. Masonite provides a wonderfully smooth surface for painting and the dhurrie will provide a focal point that is guaranteed to be a conversation piece as well!

MATERIALS

newspaper
masonite to fit the floor area
small hammer
flooring nails
utility knife
ruler
tape measure
latex paint in dusky blue, light blue and cream
1 in square-ended brush
acrylic paint in dark blue and black
decorator's brushes
masking tape
stencil cardboard or Mylar
craft knife
½ in round-ended stencil brush
clear matt varnish

1

Lay sheets of newspaper on the floor to make an even surface. Fit the first sheet of masonite into the corner nearest the door. Hammer in nails 3 in apart and ⅝ in from the edge and fasten the masonite to the existing floor.

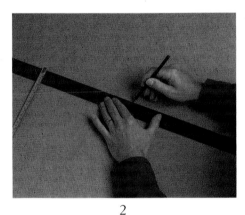

2

Lay the next sheet of masonite alongside the first, butting it hard up against the first sheet, and right up to the baseboard. Continue laying the whole boards across the room until you reach the point at which the masonite needs to be trimmed to fit. Measure the space, at least twice, if it is not too large or awkwardly shaped; if it is irregularly shaped, make a newspaper pattern to be sure of getting a good fit. Cut the masonite using a utility knife and a ruler on the shiny side, then breaking along the cut.

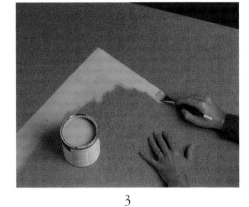

3

If you decide to place your dhurrie in the center of the room, use a tape measure to find the center line, and then measure out from it. The dhurrie can be as large or small as you like; this rug is made up of units measuring 5 × 2½ feet, which you can multiply or divide to suit your room size. Mark the outline of the dhurrie on the floor. Outline the area with the square-ended brush and then fill in the dusky blue color. Leave to dry for 2 hours.

4

Tint the blue to a darker shade by adding a squeeze of black acrylic, and then paint over the area with a dryish brush, to give the dhurrie a woven texture.

continued . . .

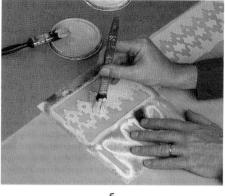

5

Trace and cut out the stencil design from the template section. Mask off the outer patterns with tape. Position the stencil ¾ in from the edge, and stencil the central design in light blue latex. Remove the tape and clean the stencil.

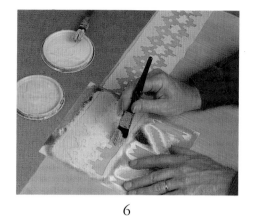

6

Now mask off the central pattern and stencil the pattern on either side in cream latex.

7

Position the medallion stencil along the edge of the border and paint all the pattern, except for the outermost lines, in dark blue acrylic. You can mask off these lines with tape, as in the previous steps.

8

Mask off the central medallion and stencil the outer lines cream.

9

Soften the dark blue of the central medallions with light dabs of light blue latex.

10

Apply at least two coats of clear varnish to the whole area.

Cork tile Checker-board Floor

Cork is a wonderful natural material that provides a warm, quiet and relatively cheap floor-covering. It has been largely confined to the kitchen and bathroom in the past, but should not be overlooked when choosing a floor for living areas.

It is important to lay cork tiles on an even surface, so nail a layer of masonite across the floorboards first. Use only floor-grade cork tiles. The unsealed tiles used here absorbed the colored varnish well; two coats of clear polyurethane varnish with a satin finish gave a protective seal. You may prefer a commercial brand of cork tile sealant.

MATERIALS

cork floor tiles
wood-stains in shades "Dark Jacobean Oak" and "Antique Pine"
large decorator's brush
cork-tile adhesive, if necessary
clear satin varnish

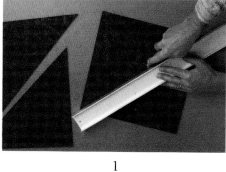

1

Paint half of the tiles with the Dark Jacobean Oak wood-stain and the remaining tiles with the Antique Pine wood-stain and leave them to dry overnight. Measure the floor length to establish the number of Jacobean Oak tiles needed and cut half that number in half diagonally. Begin laying tiles in the corner that will be seen most; then, if you have to trim a tile at the other end, it will not be so obvious. If you are using self-adhesive tiles, simply peel off the backing.

2

Lay the contrasting tiles next, tight up against the first row, wiping off any excess adhesive that has been forced up between the tiles, if you're using adhesive. Once you have laid the two rows, measure the nearest adjoining wall and cut half-tiles to fit the length of that baseboard as well. Glue these down.

3

Now, work to fill the floor space diagonally. Trim the tiles at the opposite edge to fit snugly against the baseboard. Apply two coats of clear varnish to seal the floor. It is important to make sure that the first coat is bone-dry before you apply the next one, so be patient, and let it dry overnight.

Acorn and Oak Leaf Border

A painted border can offset the austerity of plain wooden floorboards, while the pattern links different areas without dominating the room. The scale of the oak leaf pattern can be adjusted to suit the size of your room, but try to "think big" and enlarge the design to at least four times larger than life size, otherwise the impact will be lost.

Acorns and oak leaves have been used to decorate homes for hundreds of years, and they have a special place in country decorating. William Morris, the famous designer of the Arts and Crafts movement, used many country trees and plants in his patterns, and designed a wonderful wallpaper called "Acorns". Let the old saying "Tall oaks from little acorns grow" be your inspiration, and use this painted-floor border as the basis for a warm and welcoming country-style living room.

Paint the background a dark color and use paint with a matt finish as this will "hold" your outline drawings better than a satin or glossy paint. Begin at the corners and work towards the middle, using the templates as a measuring guide to work out your spacing. Once you have planned the placing of your design, work on a 24 in area at a time, using your whole arm to make the curves, not just the wrist. This way your painting will flow in a more natural way.

MATERIALS

medium-weight cardboard
spray adhesive
craft knife
masking tape
ruler
set square
latex paint in charcoal gray
decorator's brush
white china marker or chalk
white plate
gouache paint in yellow, sienna, umber, etc.
soft artist's brush
plank or long ruler
lining brush
clear matt varnish

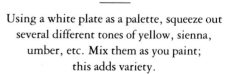

1

Use a photocopier to enlarge the oak-leaf and acorn pattern from the template section to at least four times life size (larger if you have a big room). Stick the enlargement on to medium-weight cardboard and cut around the shape with craft knife, to leave a cardboard template. Use masking tape, with a ruler and set square to outline the dark background color. Apply the color using the decorator's brush and leave to dry.

2

Beginning at the corner, draw around the oak-leaf template with the china marker or chalk. Add stems or acorns to make the pattern fit around the corner, and then continue along the border. Use the template as a measuring guide, to make sure that the design fits comfortably.

3

Using a white plate as a palette, squeeze out several different tones of yellow, sienna, umber, etc. Mix them as you paint; this adds variety.

4

Fill in the oak-leaf shapes, using subtle
variations in color for added interest.

5

Add the finishing touches and flourishes like
the leaf veining, stems and acorns.

6

Use a straight edge, such as a plank, and a
lining brush to paint the lines that enclose
the border about 1 in from the edge. Apply
3–4 coats of clear varnish, allowing generous
drying time (overnight if possible)
between coats.

Painted Canvas Floorcloth

Canvas floorcloths were first used by the early American settlers, who had traveled across the sea from Europe. They recycled canvas sailcloth, painting it to imitate the oriental carpets that were popular with the rich merchants and aristocrats in their native lands. Many layers of linseed oil were applied to the painted canvas to make them sturdy and waterproof.

The floorcloths were superseded by linoleum, and, unfortunately, few good old examples remain; they had no intrinsic value and were discarded when worn. Recently, however, they have undergone something of a revival. With the tough modern varnishes now available, they provide an unusual and sturdy alternative to the ubiquitous oriental rug.

The design for this floorcloth is based on a nineteenth-century quilt pattern called "Sun, Moon and Stars". The original quilt was made in very bright primary colors, but more muted shades work well for the floorcloth.

MATERIALS

craft knife or pair of sharp scissors
heavy artist's canvas (to order from art supply shops)
pencil
ruler
strong fabric adhesive
drawing pin and 1 yd length of string
cardboard
acrylic paint in red, blue and green
medium-size square-ended artist's brush
medium-sized pointed artist's brush
varnish in shade "Antique Pine"
household paintbrush
medium-grade sandpaper

1

Cut the canvas to the size required, allowing an extra 1½ in all around. Draw a 1½ in wide border around the edge of the canvas and miter the corners. Apply fabric adhesive to the border and fold it flat.

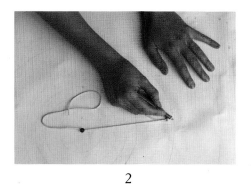

2

Referring to the diagram in the template section, find the center-point of the canvas and secure the string to the drawing pin at this point. You will now be able to draw the five circles needed for the design, by holding a pencil at various distances along the length of the tautly pulled string. Keep the tension on the string to draw a perfect circle.

3

Cut three differently sized cardboard triangles to make the saw-toothed edges of the two circles and the outside border. Just move the triangle along the pencil guidelines using the cardboard as a template to draw around.

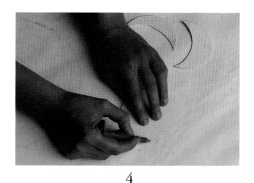

4

Cut a cardboard circle to make a template for the full moons and draw them in position. Then trim the circle to make the crescent and then the sickle moons, drawing them in position. Do the same for the stars.

5

Now start filling in the red. Use the flat-ended brush for larger areas and the pointed brush for outlines and fine work.

6

Fill in the pale blue and green circles of color.

7

Apply 3–4 coats of Antique Pine varnish with a clean household brush, rubbing down each dried coat with sandpaper before applying the next one. Overnight drying is best.

Furniture and Furnishings

....

Hand-painted furniture is all part of the country look, but unless you have the luck to inherit beautiful old pieces they often remain a distant dream. However, there are still bargains to be had from junk shops and flea markets, and they can be transformed fairly inexpensively. Renovate a table with a colorful border, paint a chair for a French country kitchen, or create your own shelves or kitchen dresser.

Country-style Motifs and Patterns

There are three main sources of motifs in country style – nature, local tradition and religion. Nature and the elements are the strongest influences of all and are celebrated in the decoration of rural homes throughout the world. Flowers and foliage vary according to climate; this is reflected in patterns and motifs, although some plants, like the vine for instance, have been used decoratively since classical times and are found in the art of many cultures.

Many fruit, flower and foliage motifs have symbolic meanings too, and these were incorporated into homes for their protective value in warding off evil, or for the bringing of good fortune. The rose is used as a symbol of love, both divine and earthly, and the tulip stands for prosperity. The oak leaf and acorn are associated with great potential and the future, while ivy symbolizes tenacity. The sunflower radiates warmth and is guaranteed to bring thoughts of summer to winter days.

Animals, birds and fish feature as well. Wild creatures, farm animals, faithful pets and feathered friends all find their way into country crafts and patterns. The rooster has been used since early Christian times as a symbol of faith, but it is more likely to feature in country

ABOVE: *The tulip is a popular folk motif, and symbolizes prosperity.*

decorating in celebration of his great decorative shape, coupled with his early-morning tyranny.

Cats and dogs are often commemorated in embroideries or paintings, as are horses and other farmyard friends. Patchwork quilts feature many animal and fruit designs that have been stylized to great effect, and this, in turn, has created a style of stenciling whose origins are the quilt-maker's patterns rather than the original inspiration.

Religious influences are especially noticeable in Roman Catholic countries, where there is more emphasis on the visual celebration of faith. Shrines, altars, festive decorations and votive offerings are all a part of the decoration of rural homes in countries like Mexico, Spain, Italy and France.

Harvest motifs, like the wheat sheaf or the cornucopia are popular in most cultures. Fruits have been incorporated into woven and printed textiles, and vegetables are a favorite subject in "theorem" paintings, a style of stencil paintings used in American folk art.

One of the most common country motifs is the heart: whether punched out of tin, carved out of planks or stenciled on to walls, the heart is everywhere. It symbolizes love and it is a uniquely simple and adaptable motif. The shape hardly changes at all, yet it can be used in many different ways without diminishing its effect. The heart has been used for many centuries across many cultures, and yet there still seems to be an infinite number of new ways to use it.

Geometric shapes have been borrowed from patchwork quilts, and suns, moons and stars will always be popular motifs. They are universal.

The beauty of country-style decorating is the nonchalance with which motifs, styles and patterns can be mixed. The only decorative effect to be avoided is mass-produced adulterated versions of country-style designs, because they will have lost their heart and soul in the manufacturing process!

LEFT: *Decorative surface detail is characteristic of country style, as in this freehand painted box.*

RIGHT: *The heart, a perennial favorite, is appliquéd in a repeat pattern on this patchwork piece.*

CLOCKWISE FROM TOP LEFT: *Stenciled details give this chair a look of pure country. Geometric patterns are always popular choices for textiles. The freehand, organic design on this box is inspired by nature. A tin heart is decorated with punched geometric patterns.*

Painted Table

It is still possible, thank goodness, to find bargain tables in junk shops, and this one cost less than a tenth of the price of a new one. It is the sort of table that you can imagine standing in a country cottage parlor, covered with a lace-edged cloth and laden with dainties. There is no guarantee that you will find a similar table, but any old table could be decorated in the same way.

Before you decorate your bargain, you may have to strip off the old paint or varnish and treat it for wood-worm, as we did. Any serious holes can be filled with wood-filler and then sanded and stained to match. The trick is to emphasize the good features and play down the bad. Old tabletops look more interesting than new ones and are well worth sanding, bleaching and staining to enhance the natural grain.

The stain on the table legs contrasts well with the red and green paint used on the tabletop. The lining can be attempted freehand, but masking tape makes the job much easier. Mark the position lightly in pencil so that all the lines are the same distance from the edge.

MATERIALS

*table,
wood-stain in shade "Dark Jacobean Oak"
household paintbrush
latex paint in red and green
1/2 in square-ended artist's brush
masking tape
shellac
beeswax polish
soft clean cloth*

1

Prepare and treat the table as necessary. Use a rag to rub the wood stain into the table legs, applying more as it is absorbed into the wood. The finish should be an even, almost black tone.

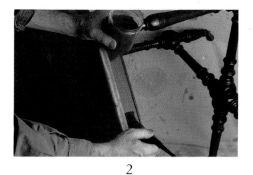

2

Paint the base of the table-top with red latex.

3

Measure 2 in in from the edge of the table and place a strip of masking tape this distance in from each of the edges. Leave a ¾ inch gap and then place the next strips of tape to run parallel with the first set.

4

Fill in the strip between the tape with the green paint and let dry.

5

Apply two coats of shellac to the table.

6

Finish the table with a coat of beeswax polish, buffing it to a warm sheen with a soft clean cloth.

Painted Chest

Before the eighteenth century, throughout northern Europe and Scandinavia, a country bride took her own decorated linen chest into her new home. The dowry chest would have been made by her father, lovingly carved and painted as a farewell gift to his daughter. Marriage customs accounted for many rural crafts, and the family took great pride in providing a handsome chest for a bride. This custom was continued among the first settlers in North America.

The chest used in this project is a mixture of Old and New World influences. The shape is English, but the painted decoration was inspired by an old American dowry chest. The pattern used on the chest is geometric, but the paint finish is very loosely applied, to give a good contrast between two styles. You can use the pattern to decorate any blanket chest, old or new, and then give it an antique finish with tinted varnish.

The most time-consuming aspect is the accurate drawing up of the pattern shapes, but it is worth spending time to get the proportions right. The combing and spotting has to be done quickly, so the effect is one of controled chaos!

MATERIALS

blanket chest
shellac,. if necessary
latex paint in dusky blue
and cream
household paintbrushes
tracing paper
pair of compasses
ruler
acrylic varnish in shade
"Antique Pine"
graining comb
clean damp cloth

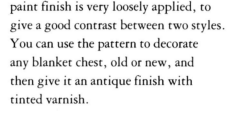

1

If you are starting with bare wood, apply a coat of shellac to seal the surface.

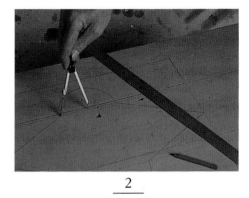

2

Paint the chest with dusky blue latex. Trace and enlarge the pattern from the template section and use it as a guide to position the panels. Draw the panels with a pair of compasses and ruler.

3

Fill in all the panels with cream latex.

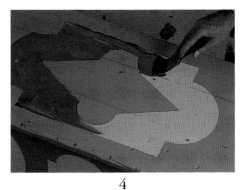

4

Apply a thick coat of varnish to one panel only.

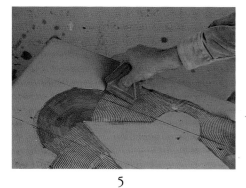

5

Quickly comb the varnish in a pattern, following the shape of the panel. Make one smooth combing movement into the wet varnish, and then wipe the comb to prevent any buildup of varnish. Complete one panel before repeating steps 4 and 5 for the other panels.

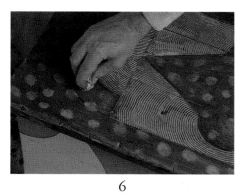

6

Apply a coat of varnish to the whole chest. Immediately take a just-damp cloth, crumple it into a ball and use it to dab off spots of the varnish.

Painted Bench

Every home should have a bench like this, to squeeze extra guests around the dinner table and to keep by the back door for comfortable boot-changing. This bench was made by a carpenter, from a photograph seen in a book of old country furniture. The wood is reclaimed floorboards, which give just the right rustic feel to the bench.

The decoration is applied in a rough folk-art style that adds a touch of humor. You can use this style to decorate any bench, and even a plain modern design will lose its hard edges and take on the character of a piece of rustic handmade furniture.

MATERIALS

bench
medium-grade sandpaper
shellac
household paintbrushes
latex paint in deep red,

dark blue-gray and light
blue-green
small piece of sponge
varnish in shade "Antique Pine"
clear matt varnish

1

Sand the bare wood and seal it with a coat of shellac.

2

Paint the legs in dark blue-gray latex, working directly on to the wood.

3

Paint the seat with the deep red latex.

4

Use the sponge to dab an even pattern of blue-green spots across the whole surface of the seat.

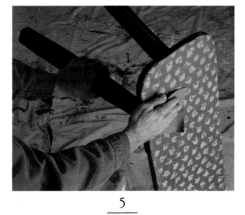

5

When the paint is dry, rub the seat and edges with sandpaper, to simulate the wear and tear of a thousand harvest dinners.

6

Apply one coat of Antique Pine varnish to the whole bench. Then apply two more coats of matt varnish for a strong finish.

Shaker-inspired Peg Rail

The Shakers were a religious movement whose ideals inspired a style of furnishings and furniture of great simplicity and beauty of form. They did not believe in ornamentation or decoration for its own sake, but held that functional objects should be as beautiful and as well made as possible. The name "Shaker" comes from the ecstatic movements that occurred in their worship.

Peg rails were very characteristic of Shaker homes, and were used for hanging all kinds of utensils and even chairs, keeping the floor clear. Our rail is a very inexpensive and simplified version of the Shaker idea, and what it lacks in fine craftsmanship it makes up for in practicality. We have used a pine plank, with a sawn-off broom handle to make the pegs. These rails work well all around the house, but are especially useful in hallways, children's rooms and bathrooms. The coat of paint is not strictly Shaker in style, but will disguise the rail's humble origins.

MATERIALS

pine plank 1 in thick
ruler
saw
plane
drill with bit for broom
handle holes
1 or 2 broom handles
medium-grade sandpaper
wood glue

wooden block and hammer
shellac
household paintbrushes
latex paint in dusky blue
varnish in shade "Antique Pine"
paint thinner, if necessary
carpenter's level
wall-fixings and long screws

1

Measure and cut the wood to the length required. Plane it to smooth and round the edges.

2

Mark the peg positions 8 in apart along the length. The spacing can be altered to suit your requirements.

3

Drill holes ⅝ in deep in which to recess the pegs.

4

Cut up the broom handles into 5 in lengths. Sand the edges to round them off.

<u>5</u>

Apply wood glue and fit the pegs into their holes using a small wood block and hammer to fit them tightly.

<u>6</u>

Apply one coat of shellac to seal the surface of the wood.

<u>7</u>

Paint the rail blue.

<u>8</u>

Use medium-grade sandpaper to rub back to bare wood along the edges.

<u>9</u>

Give the whole shelf a coat of Antique Pine varnish. Dip a rag in paint thinner (for polyurethane varnish) or water (for acrylic varnish) and rub off some of the varnish. Use a carpenter's level and ruler to mark the position of the rail on the wall. Drill holes through the rail at 18 in intervals. Drill into the wall, using suitable wall-fixings and screws.

Painted and Lined Country Chair

It is always worth buying interesting individual chairs when you spot them, as they are often very inexpensive if they need refinishing. Four mismatched chairs painted the same way will make a convincing and charming set, and the effect is pure country.

This is a typical French country style, rush-seated chair, with curvaceous lines just begging to be accentuated with lining. The essentials of sturdiness and comfort have not been ignored, the seat is generously woven and it is very comfortable. (It is always worth sitting on your chair before you buy because it may have been custom-made for a differently shaped person!)

Color is a real revitalizer and we have chosen a yellow and blue color scheme reminiscent of the painter Monet's kitchen, to bring out the French character of the chair. It is worth spending time preparing the wood, and this may mean stripping all the paint if there are several layers of gloss. If you do have the chair professionally stripped, the joints will need to be re-glued, because the caustic stripper dissolves glue as well as paint.

MATERIALS

country-style chair
medium-grade sandpaper
undercoat
household paintbrushes
shellac and wood primer,
if necessary
latex paint in yellow
wire wool
hard pencil
tube of artist's oil color in
ultramarine blue
paint thinner
long-haired square-ended
artist's brush
varnish in shade "Antique Pine"

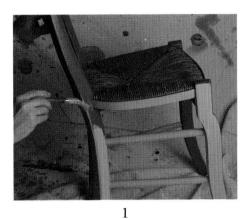

1

If the chair hasn't been stripped, rub it down well with medium-grade sandpaper. Apply the undercoat, or if the chair has been stripped, give it a coat of shellac followed by wood primer. Paint the chair yellow.

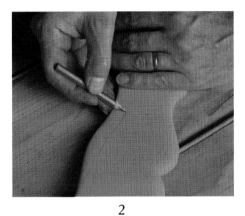

2

When this coat has dried, use wire wool to rub the paint back along the edges where natural wearing away would take place. With a pencil draw the lining, following the curves of the chair.

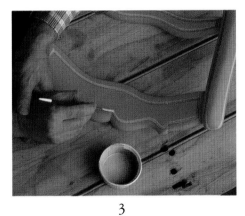

3

Mix the oil paint with paint thinner in the proportions 3 parts paint to 1 part paint thinner. You need paint that flows smoothly from the brush and allows you to retain control. If you find the paint too runny, add more color. Practice the brushstroke with the artist's brush on scrap paper or board, supporting your brush-hand with your spare hand. Controling your lines is a matter of confidence, which grows as you paint. Paint the lining on the legs, chairback and seat.

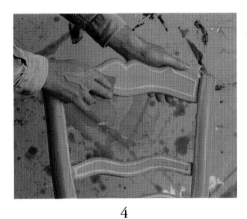

4

When dry, rub back with wire wool in places, as you did with the yellow.

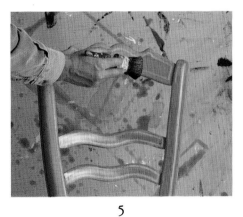

5

Finally apply a coat or two of varnish to soften the color and protect the lining.

Pie-safe Cupboard

Cupboards like this one were mainly used in America as cooling cupboards for freshly baked goods. The doors were made out of decoratively punched and pierced tin sheets that allowed the delicious aromas to waft out, but prevented flies from getting in. They were called "safes" because they were fitted with locks to keep temptation out of reach of little fingers lured by delicious smells!

We used an existing old pine cupboard to make the pie-safe, replacing the wooden front panels with newly pierced tin ones. Milled-steel sheet can be bought from sheet-metal suppliers, or try asking at a hardware store or looking in Yellow Pages. Care must be taken, as the edges of the sheet are very sharp, and need to be folded over to make a safe seam. You can crimp or flatten the edges using pliers.

The actual patterning is done with a hammer and nail, or, for more linear piercing, you can use a small chisel. This pattern is our own interpretation of a traditional design, but once you begin, your own style will emerge. You may find other ways of making patterns, perhaps using the end of a Phillips screwdriver, for instance – really anything goes. If the cupboard is to be used in the kitchen, add a protective backing sheet behind the tin, to cover the sharp edges. To get rid of the very new gleam of pierced metal, rub vinegar into the surface.

MATERIALS

old cupboard with one or two paneled doors
tracing paper
medium-grade sandpaper
shellac, if necessary
24- or 26-gauge milled-steel sheet(s) to fit (allow ½ in all around for the seams)
pliers and tin snips, if necessary
masking tape
pair of compasses or transfer paper
china marker
hammer
selection of different nails, screwdrivers and chisels
backing material such as masonite, if necessary
panel pins
varnish in shade "Antique Pine"
household paintbrush

1

Remove any beading and ease out the existing panels from the cupboard doors. Measure the space and use tracing paper to plan the design to fit. Rub down the cupboard with sandpaper. If it has been stripped, re-seal it with a coat of shellac. Trim the metal sheet, if necessary. Fold over the sharp edge of the metal sheet, to make a seam about ½ in deep around the edge. Crimp firmly with pliers. Put masking tape over sharp edges, to prevent accidental cuts.

2

Transfer your design on to the tin surface, using a pair of compasses. If you find this tricky, trace the whole design and use transfer paper to put it on to the metal. Add any extra designs with the china marker.

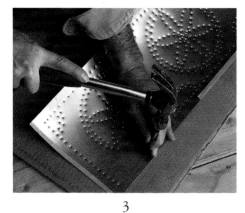

3

Practice piercing on a scrap of tin, such as a cookie-tin lid, so that you know how hard you need to hit the nail to pierce a hole, and also how just to dent the surface without piercing it. Place thick cardboard or an old towel or blanket beneath the tin to absorb the noise and protect the surface underneath. Once you are confident with the hammer and nail, or whatever tool you want to use, hammer out the pattern.

4

Fit the pierced panels, and the backing if you are using it, into the door and replace the beading to secure it. Use short panel pins at a distance of 1½ in apart, all around the panel to fix in place.

5

Sandpaper the edges to simulate a time worn effect. Give the wood a protective coat of varnish.

Shelf with Hanging Hooks

This large shelf with a backboard and hooks would suit a kitchen, entrance hall or large bathroom. It is really simple to make, requiring only the most basic of carpentry skills and tools. The shelf can be painted or varnished, depending on the wood, and it's a really handsome and useful piece of furniture.

The very best wood to use is reclaimed pine, usually floorboards. Demolition or builder's reclamation yards usually have stocks of old wood, but be prepared to pay more for old than new pine. If you're leaving the shelf unpainted it's definitely worth the extra money for old wood. If you intend to paint the shelf, new wood can be used for the backing board, to cut down on the price.

The best feature of the shelf is the very generously sized brackets, which were copied from an old farm storeroom. They have been cut from a section of old pine door, using a jig saw. The brackets will support the shelf and balance the weight, but the shelf should be screwed into a sound brick wall, using suitable wall fixings and long steel screws.

This type of shelf is very popular in rural eastern European communities. The hooks can either be new brass or wrought-iron coathooks; or you may be lucky enough to find an old set. Either way they are bound to be concealed, as hooks usually attract more than they were ever intended to hold!

MATERIALS

tracing paper
piece of pine
14½ in × 7 in × 1¼ in thick, for the brackets
jig saw
drill with No. 5 and 6 bits
pine plank 3 ft 4 in × 6 in × ¾ in thick, for the backboard
pine plank 4 ft 4 in × 8½ in × ¾ in thick, for the shelf
wood glue
wood-screws
shellac
household paintbrush
1 in brush
latex paint in dusky blue, sky blue and jade
clean damp cloth
steel wool
medium-grade sandpaper
6 coathooks
wall fixings, if necessary
3 long screws

1

Trace the bracket pattern from the template section and enlarge it until the longest side measures 13½ in. Trace this on to the wood, fitting it into one corner, and then flip the pattern over and trace it again into the opposite-end corner. The two can be cut out at the same time, using a jig saw. Use the number 5 drill bit to make two holes through the backboard into the brackets; and also through the shelf down into the brackets. Spread wood glue on all the joining edges, and then screw them together with wood-screws.

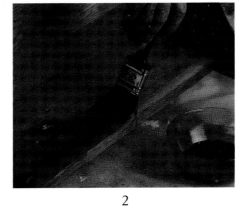

2

Apply one coat of shellac to the whole unit.

3

Use the 1 in brush to apply a coat of dusky blue latex.

4

When dry, apply a coat of sky blue.

5

Immediately afterwards, use a damp cloth to
wipe the paint off in some areas.

6

Paint the edges of the shelf and brackets
with jade.

7

Rub away some of the dried paint using steel
wool. This will reveal the wood grain along
the edges.

8

Finally rub down with medium-grade
sandpaper to smooth the finish and reveal the
grain. Screw in the hooks. Attach to the wall
by drilling through the backboard to make
holes for long wood-screws. Use suitable
wall fixings, if necessary.

Painted Dresser

If there is one item of furniture that typifies country style in most people's minds, it must surely be the dresser. A sturdy cupboard topped with china-laden shelves is an irresistible sight.

This dresser was made by a local carpenter using reclaimed pine, but a dresser can easily be made up using a sturdy chest of drawers combined with a set of bookshelves. The trick is to make sure that the two are balanced visually, with the height and depth of the shelves suiting the width of the base. You can join the two unobtrusively by using strong steel brackets at the back, and painting will complete the illusion that the two were made for each other.

The washed-out paint finish is achieved by using no undercoat and rubbing the dried paint down to the wood with sandpaper and steel wool. Alternatively you can rub some areas of the wood with candle wax before you begin painting; the candle wax will resist the paint, leaving the wood bare.

MATERIALS

dresser, or combination of shelves and base cupboard
shellac
household paintbrushes
latex paint in dusky blue, brick
red (optional), and cream
household candle (optional)
medium-grade sandpaper and steel wool
varnish in shade "Antique Pine"

1

Apply a coat of shellac to seal the bare wood.

2

Paint the dresser dusky blue, following the direction of the grain. Allow to dry.

3

If desired, rub candle wax along the edges of the dresser before painting with a second color.

4

The wax will prevent the second color from adhering completely, and will create a distressed effect. Add the second color, if using.

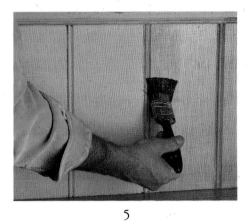

5

Paint the backing boards cream, again following the direction of the grain.

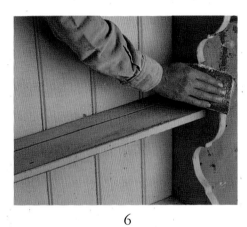

6

When the paint has dried, use medium-grade sandpaper and steel wool to rub down to bare wood along the edges, to simulate wear and tear.

7

Finally apply a coat of Antique Pine varnish to the whole dresser to protect the surface.

Details and Accessories

....

Little details complete the country interior — candle sticks or sconces holding beeswax candles; shelves decorated with lace, ribbon or punched leather; brightly painted tins stocking the pantry; and baskets, copper pans, and dried flowers hung from butcher's hooks, making a delightful display in the kitchen. These ideas, and more, are all simple to make and will transform your home.

Finishing Touches

Once you have transformed your home with country-style paint finishes, furniture and flooring, it is time to add the finishing touches. The accumulation of "finds" that add personality to a home does take time, and should be a gradual process; it often depends on your being in the right place at the right time. An unlimited supply of money would buy you folk art treasures and an interior-designed country look, but you would certainly miss out on the pleasure of making your own accessories.

There are projects in this section to suit most talents and skills, whether your talent lies with a needle and thread, carpenter's tools or paintbrushes.

A simple broom handle can be used to display a collection of baskets hanging from the ceiling and découpage transforms any ordinary tray into one to be displayed on the wall as "art".

Shelving can be dressed up with lace, ribbons, paper or even punched leather, to make something functional into a decorative feature. It is well worth seeking out a local carpenter if you lack

ABOVE: *This punched-tin sconce creates a wonderful backdrop for candles.*

the space or inclination to make your own shelving, because reclaimed timber like pine floorboarding is really worth using for its character and color.

Candlelight is essential for adding a cosy atmosphere, and whether you choose to make the baluster candlesticks or the rustic wall sconce, you will be enriching the room with something unusual and handmade. Use the ideas suggested as a starting point, adding your own color schemes and patterns to give each thing you make a personal touch.

The embroidered valance looks very special, and the shapes do not require any particular needlecraft skill to follow. A simple chain stitch could be used to outline all the shapes, and satin stitch for the scallops. The more advanced embroiderer could elaborate upon the designs, filling the background as well as the kitchen implements with a variety of colors and fancy stitchwork.

Similarly, the patchwork throw does not need any more than basic sewing-machine skills to fit it together. The design will vary, depending on your selection of warm winter scarves and backing fabric, and the more experienced seamstress will be tempted to make the pattern more complicated by adding differently shaped patches. Whether you choose to make the basic throw or a more complicated variation, you are bound to be delighted with the result. It looks great draped over a chair and is wonderfully warm and insulating on a cold country evening.

There are many country crafts that can be studied and mastered, like basket-making, weaving or the carving of decoy ducks. If you have time to explore and learn about how things are traditionally made, it is very enriching. Our projects are more about taking short cuts and making an impact, which is a good creative starting point. Once you realize the pleasure that is to be gained from both making and displaying your own creations, you are bound to continue to experiment and to enjoy country crafts.

LEFT AND RIGHT: *Warmth and beauty are the keynotes of any country kitchen. Utensils are displayed within easy reach, and dried goods may be kept in colorfully painted tins.*

CLOCKWISE FROM TOP LEFT: *A painted salt box, Shaker-style doll and varnished trug all add a feeling of country. Candles complete the scene. Sewing odds and ends can be kept neat in a wooden box. These pinwheels form an eye-catching still-life with a collection of plates in complementary colors. A color-washed tin lantern sets off a display of beeswax candles.*

Wall Sconce

These fashionable room accessories were once essential to every household; however, one wonders what our ancestors would make of us forsaking the convenience of electricity for the "romance" of candlelight. The truth is that technology and mass-production seem to take the humanity out of our homes, making us long for the irregularity of candlelight, hand-stitching and country-crafted furniture.

MATERIALS

old piece of wood, preferably
driftwood
saw
hammer
brass and black upholstery nails
wood glue
nails

1

Saw through the wood, making two sections to be joined at right angles. Begin the pattern by hammering the upholstery nails in a central line; the pattern can then radiate from it.

2

Form arrows, diamonds and crosses, using the contrast between the brass and black tacks to enhance your design.

3

Apply a coating of wood glue to the sawn edge of the base. Hammer fine nails through the back into the base.

Découpage Tray

A good tray will be strong enough to carry mugs and plates and handsome enough to hang up as a decoration when not in use. This one has been découpaged with a selection of old engraving tools, but you could follow the method using any design you choose.

Découpage takes you back to childhood; cutting out and gluing is a favorite activity of children between the ages of five and ten. The grown up version is slightly more sophisticated, but the fun remains.

The secret of good découpage lies in accurate cutting and in putting on enough coats of varnish. Serious enthusiasts use 30 layers, rubbing down with fine sandpaper between the coats. The idea is to bring the background up to the level of the applied decoration, and then to add further depth with more coats, possibly to include crackle glaze and antique varnish. The final result should be convincing to both eye and touch.

MATERIALS

tray
woodwash in corn yellow
household paintbrush
fine-grade sandpaper
photocopied motifs to cut out
sharp-pointed scissors or utility knife
wallpaper paste and brush
soft cloth
new paintbrush for varnishing
clear satin varnish
crackle glaze (optional)
artist's oil paint in raw umber

1

Prepare the tray by painting it with corn yellow as a base color. When dry, rub the surface with fine-grade sandpaper.

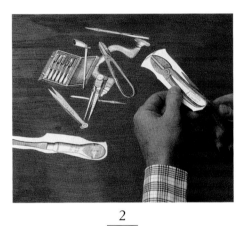

2

Cut out your paper shapes carefully, moving the paper towards the scissors, or around on the cutting surface, so that you are always using the scissors or utility knife in the most comfortable and fluid way.

3

Turn the cut-outs over and paste the backs with wallpaper paste, right up to all the edges, covering the entire area.

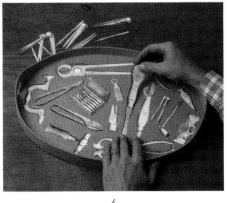

4

Glue them down in position on the tray.

continued . . .

DETAILS AND ACCESSORIES

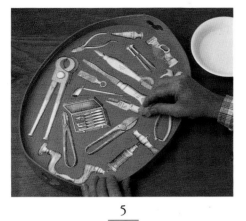

5

Use a soft cloth to smooth out any bubbles.
Leave to dry overnight.

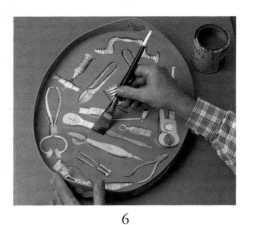

6

Begin varnishing, using a clean new brush
and applying a sparing coat to the whole
surface of the tray. When dry, rub lightly
with fine-grade sandpaper and repeat as many
times as possible.

7

A further dimension has been added to this
découpage, by the application of a crackle
glaze. There are several brands on the
market. It is best to follow the specific
instructions for the product you use.
Here the base varnish is being painted
on to the tray.

8

When this coat is dry (after 20 minutes),
apply an even coat of crackle glaze and leave
it to dry for 20 minutes.

9

Rub a small amount of artist's oil paint into
the cracks, using a cotton cloth. Raw umber
was used here, which gives a naturally aged
effect but any color can be used.

10

When the cracks have been colored,
gently rub the excess paint from the surface,
using a soft cloth.

11

Give the tray at least two more coats of clear
satin varnish; many more if time and
patience allow.

Wooden Candlesticks

This pair of matching wooden candlesticks have been made from old balusters that were removed from a stair rail. This is an easy way to make something from turned wood without having to operate a lathe yourself. Balusters can be bought singly from lumber yards, hardware stores or home centers.

The only special equipment needed is a vise and a flat-head drill bit, to make a hole in the top of the baluster large enough to hold a candle.

The candlesticks have been painted in bright earthy colors, giving a matching pair fit to grace any country table.

MATERIALS

saw
2 wooden balusters (reclaimed or new)
2 square wood scraps
medium- and fine-grade sandpaper
wood glue
vise

electric drill fitted with a flat-head drill bit
acrylic paint in bright yellow, red and raw umber or burnt sienna
household and artist's brushes
acrylic clear matt varnish
soft clean cloth

1

Cut out the most interesting section of the baluster and a square base; this one measures 3 × 3 in. Roughen the bottom of the baluster with sandpaper.

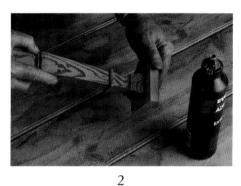

2

Very slightly, bevel the base with fine-grade sandpaper. Glue the two sections together with wood glue.

3

Hold the candlestick securely in the vise and drill a hole for the candle 3¾ in in diameter and ¾ in deep.

4

Paint with two or three coats of bright yellow acrylic paint.

5

Apply a coat of orange acrylic paint (add a touch of red to the yellow acrylic).

6

Tint the varnish to a muddy brown, by adding a squeeze of raw umber or burnt sienna. Brush this over the orange.

7

Use a crumpled cloth to lift some varnish and reveal the color below.

Woolen Patchwork Throw

Believe it or not, this stunning chair throw cost next to nothing to make, and was finished in an afternoon! It is made from pure woolen scarves and remnant wool fabric. The scarves come from thrift shops, and can be bought for pennies. To simplify your design choose a color scheme derived from your remnant. The throw is lined with a length of old brocade curtain, but a flannel sheet would also be suitable, especially if you dyed it a dark color.

The only skill you need for this project is the ability to sew a straight line on a sewing machine: and plaid scarves provide good guidelines to follow. Clear a good space on the floor and lay the fabric and scarves out, moving them around until you are happy with the color combinations. You may refer to the diagram in the template section for the basic pattern, but you will probably want to adapt it somewhat to suit your choice of colors. Cut out the first central square. The diamond shape will need to be hemmed and tacked before you sew it to the center of the first square; after this, each strip of scarf will just need to be pinned and sewn in position.

The throw could easily be adapted to make a bedcover, and, because of the fine-quality wool used for scarves, it will be exceptionally warm. The challenge with this throw is to resist draping yourself in it, instead of the chair!

DETAILS AND ACCESSORIES

....

MATERIALS

scissors
about 1 yd wool fabric
selection of plaid and plain
woolen scarves
pins, thread and sewing machine
old curtain or flannel sheet,
for lining

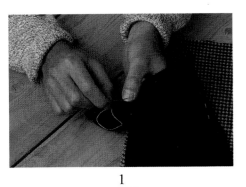

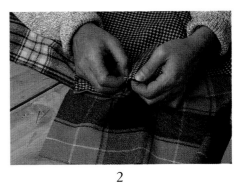

1

Cut out a 18 × 18 in square of your "background" fabric. Choose the pattern for your central diamond and cut a square, using the width of the scarf as the measurement for the sides. Turn the edges under ½ in and baste. Pin and sew the diamond in position.

2

Choose two scarves and cut them into four rectangles. Position them along the sides of the square, with the matching patterns facing each other. Sew them in place and trim off any excess.

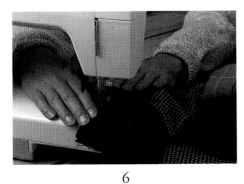

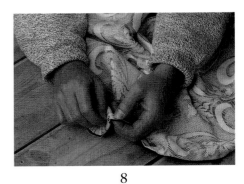

3

Cut out four matching plain squares and pin and sew them into the corners. Check on the right side, to make sure that the corners meet accurately. Cut four strips of the background fabric to fit the sides, about 5½ in wide.

4

Cut out four corner pieces of the scarf used for the central diamond, 5½ in × 5½ in. Sew a square to one end of each strip of background fabric.

5

Pin and then sew these long strips in position around the edge of the patchwork.

6

Cut a plain scarf into four strips lengthwise and sew these around the outside edge, overlapping at the corners to complete the square.

7

Cut the lining to fit and sew the two pieces together, with their right sides facing inwards.

8

Turn inside out and sew up the seam by hand. Press, using a damp cloth and dry iron.

Braided "Rag Rug" Tie-backs

Tie-backs are an attractive way of getting the maximum amount of daylight into the house. It is surprising how much difference a few inches more exposure of windowpanes can make to the light in a room, so unless your windows are huge, it is well worth tying your curtains back into the wall. This idea has a real hands-on feel and can be made to coordinate or contrast with existing curtains.

This method of braiding scraps of fabric has been stolen from rag-rug makers, and if you have always wanted to make one, this may be just the introduction that you need! If you have any fabric left over from your curtains, you could incorporate this into the braids. If not, one plain color that appears in your curtains will have a harmonizing effect on the whole scheme.

MATERIALS

*scraps of fabric cut into
3-in wide strips
safety pin
needle and thread
scissors
strip of fabric for backing (one for
each tie-back)
2 D-rings for each tie-back*

1

Roll up the fabric strips, leaving a workable length unfurled.

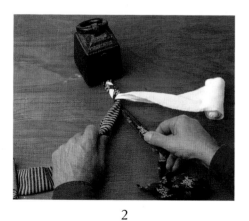

2

Join three strips together, rolling one fabric around the other two and pinning them together with the safety pin. Attach the ends to a chair or any suitable stationary object or anchor them under a heavy weight. Begin braiding, rolling the strips into tubes as you go, so that the rough edges are turned in and concealed. Make tight braids. The tie-back needs to be at least 20 in long and four braids deep.

3

The thickness and length depend on the fabric you will be tying back, but this is an average measurement. Work until you have the required length and number of braids. Lay the braids flat and sew the edges together using a large needle and heavy-duty thread pulled up tight. Keep the braids flat when you turn at either end.

4

Cut a backing strip, allowing enough fabric to turn under ⅝ in all round. Attach the D rings at either end as you slip-stitch the lining into place.

Quilted Tie-backs

This is a quilting project for the absolute beginner. All that is required is the ability to sew an even running stitch along a drawn line. The pattern is a standard quilting stencil (available from craft shops), which you draw through using a chalky colored pencil. A layer of batting is placed between two strips of fabric, which can then be basted or pinned together.

The effect produced by the quilting is textural and the pattern shows up very well. The quilting is best done on plain fabrics, like the one we used, but the tie-backs could be used with patterned curtains. Gingham or larger checked patterns look especially good teamed with quilted muslin.

MATERIALS

1 yd unbleached cotton fabric
scissors
20 in quilter's
batting
quilt stencil pattern
chalky colored pencil
pins, needle and thread
2 D-rings for each tie-back

1

Cut the calico into strips 20 in × 5¾ in. Cut the batting into strips 19 in × 4 in. Use the stencil to draw on to one piece of fabric. Put a layer of batting in between two layers of fabric and pin.

2

Sew a running stitch along the pattern lines. You may find it easiest to pull the needle through each time, rather than sewing in and out of all three layers at once.

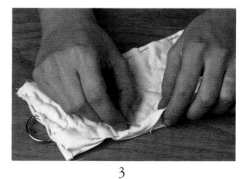

3

When the pattern is complete, fold in the edges and stitch them all around, either by hand or machine. Attach a D-ring at each end.

Leather-edged Shelf Trimming

Not all shelves are worthy of display, especially the new and inexpensive ones that are readily available in hardware stores. There is no denying that they are practical and functional, but a simple shelf trimming will transform them very quickly into a charming and individual room feature.

MATERIALS

*leather scraps (sold by weight
in craft shops)
round template with a 3 in
diameter
pencil, ruler and chalk
pinking shears
multi-sized hole punch
double-sided tape or glue*

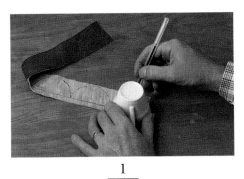

1

Cut strips of leather to fit the length of your shelf, using several sections to make up the length if necessary. The edging needs to be 2½ in deep. Draw a line ½ in from the edge (on the reverse side) and use the template to draw semi-circles along the length of the line.

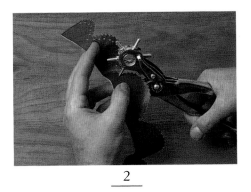

2

Cut around these with pinking shears. Punch out holes around the edges, varying the sizes.

3

Draw stars on the semi-circles with chalk. Punch out holes around the star outlines in the same way. Run a strip of double-sided tape along the shelf, and use this to attach the leather trim; alternatively all-purpose glue can be used.

Lace and Gingham Shelf Trimming

The lacy look may not suit every room, but it can add a very French touch to a dresser or kitchen shelf. The contrast between stout enamel pans and fine cotton lace can be quite charming; in French country homes, crochet lace is pinned up for display on any shelf available.

There are so many different lace designs available, that the decision will have to be a personal one. You may go for an antique hand-crocheted piece or a simpler machine-made design. The pointed edging chosen here suits a china display very well.

There is something both cheerful and practical about gingham. It is perfectly suited to edging food-cupboard shelves, where the pattern is strong enough to stand out against all the different packaging designs. The combination with lace is fresh and pretty.

MATERIALS

strips of lace the length of the cupboard shelves, plus extra for turnings
cold tea
small bowl

scissors
double-sided tape
gingham ribbon the length of the sides of the shelves
all-purpose glue

1

To tone down the brightness of this new lace, it was dipped into a bowl of cold tea. The stronger the brew, the darker the color, so adjust it by adding water to lighten the dye, if necessary. Press the lace when dry and cut it to the correct length.

2

Apply the double-sided tape to the vertical sides of the shelves and peel off the backing tape. Cut the gingham ribbon to fit and seal the ends with a little glue, which will dry clear and prevent the ends from fraying.

3

Stick the gingham ribbon to the verticals, carefully smoothing it out and keeping it straight. Start at one end, and keep the ribbon taut.

4

Apply double-sided tape to the edges of the shelves, overlapping the gingham.

5

Seal one end of the lace with a small amount of glue. Stretch it along the tape, cut it to fit and seal the edge. Repeat for the other shelves.

DETAILS AND ACCESSORIES

French Bread Box

*The kitchen and meal times play a central role in country life, entailing warm
winter suppers when the nights have drawn in, or long, languorous lunches
in the height of summer. Crusty bread is an integral part of any meal, and
this stylish bread box will bring a touch of French country style to your kitchen.
The same design could be used in a hallway or by the back door
to hold umbrellas or canes.*

The pattern provided in the template
section could be given to a carpenter, or,
if woodworking is a hobby, made at
home. The stand has been made from
reclaimed pine floorboards, which are
quite heavy and give it stability, as does
the molding used to broaden the base.

The decoration is called ferning and was
very popular in Victorian times. Dried or
imitation ferns (florist's sell fake plastic
or silk ones) are sprayed with spray
mount and arranged on the surface,
which is then spray painted. It dries very
quickly and the ferns can then be lifted
off. The effect is stunning and very easy
to achieve.

MATERIALS

wood for the stand (see pattern)
tracing paper or transfer paper
jig saw or coping saw
wood glue and 1 in nails
hammer

For the decoration
shellac
household paintbrush
newspaper
masking tape
spray mount
selection of artificial ferns
spray paint in black, dark green
or dark blue
fine-grade sandpaper
clear matt varnish

1

Apply two coats of shellac to seal and color
the bare wood.

TO MAKE THE STAND

Cut the wood to the dimensions shown
on the pattern in the template section.
Miter the edges. Trace the
pattern for the back detail and cut it out
using a jig saw or coping saw.
Apply wood glue to all joining edges,
join them and then use nails
to secure them.

2

Working on one side at a time, mask off the
surrounding area with newspaper and masking
tape. Apply spray mount to one side
of the ferns and arrange them on the surface.

3

Spray on the color, using light, even sprays,
and building up the color gradually.
Lift the ferns when the paint is dry.

72

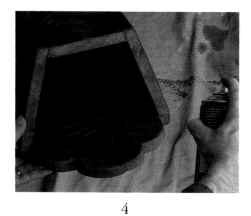

4

Work on all the sides and the inside back panel in the same way.

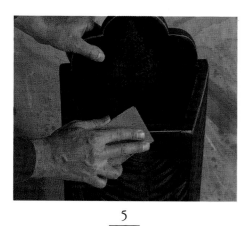

5

Sand the edges to simulate a timeworn look.

6

Finally, apply two coats of varnish to protect the fernwork.

Rabbit Dummy Board

A freestanding oversized rabbit will certainly provide both a focal point and a conversation piece! Dummy boards originated as shop or inn signs; in the days when few people could read, a painted sign would indicate the trade being practiced on the premises. The signs would either hang above the doorway or stand on a wooden block. You can give this rabbit a support to make it stand up, or hang it on the wall.

This project employs a mixture of old and new, as it is an original nineteenth-century engraving enlarged on a photocopier. The fine lines of the original thicken up with enlargement, but not enough to lose the effect of an engraving.

This project is great fun and fairly simple, and the only real skill required is that of cutting the shape out with a jig saw. Personal experience has shown us that there are people who delight in this; so if you don't have a jig saw – find someone who does!

MATERIALS

wallpaper paste and brush
23¾ × 16¾ in sheet of marine
plywood (or similar)
jig saw
fine-grade sandpaper
shellac
household paintbrushes
varnish in shade "Antique Pine"
clear matt varnish
scrap of wood for stand
white glue

___1___

Photocopy the rabbit pattern from the template section, enlarging it to the edges of an 8½ × 11 in sheet. Cut the enlargement in two equal halves.

___2___

Enlarge both of these up to 11 × 17 in. Depending on the machine, this process can be done in one step, or might take several enlargements.

___3___

Apply a coat of wallpaper paste to the plywood. This seals the surface and provides a base for the pasted paper.

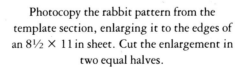

___4___

Trim the "joining" edges of the photocopies right up to the print, so that they can butt up against each other with no overlap. Apply a thin layer of wallpaper paste right up to the edges and stick the two halves together on the board. Smooth out any bubbles with a soft cloth and leave it to dry overnight.

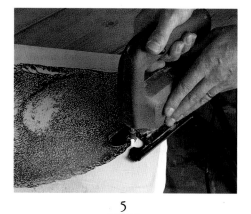

5

Use a jig saw to cut out the shape, leaving a flat base. Using a jig saw is not difficult, but you will need to practice to get the feel of it. Take your time.

6

Sand the edges of the rabbit smooth.

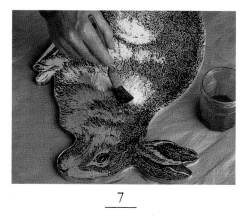

7

Seal the surface with a coat of shellac, which will give it a yellowish glow. Apply a coat of Antique Pine varnish, followed by several coats of clear varnish.

8

Trace the pattern from the template section to the final size 6½ × 5½ × 1½ in. Use it to cut out the stand. Rub down the edges with fine-grade sandpaper and glue in place.

Painted Tin or Tôleware

Tin-painting reached its zenith in the early days of American settlement, when itinerant merchants would appear in a blaze of color at farm gates, selling their decorated tin housewares. Even then, they were hard to resist and most homes boasted a display of painted tinware. The word "tôleware" derives from the French tôle peinté *meaning "painted tin", but the style of painting owes more to the Norwegian* rosemaling *than the elaborate French style.*

Our project does not require you to learn the specialized brushstrokes used in traditional tin-painting, although the colors and antiquing will ensure that it blends in well with any other tôleware pieces. These numbered tins were used by tea merchants as containers for different tea blends.

MATERIALS

metal primer
household paintbrushes
large metal can (either tin or
aluminum) with a lid
latex paint in black,
brick-red and corn yellow
small artist's brush
tracing paper (optional)
soft pencil
masking tape
selection of artist's brushes
hard pencil
shellac
clear varnish tinted with
raw umber acrylic paint
clear satin varnish

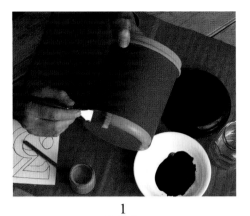

1

Prime the can. Paint the lid with black
latex and the can brick-red, with bands
of corn yellow.

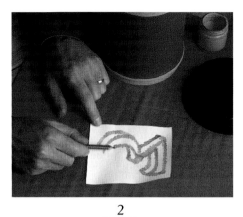

2

Trace or photocopy the pattern from the
template section up to a suitable size
and then cross-hatch over the back with
a soft pencil.

3

Use low-tack masking tape to hold the
pattern in position and then draw over it
with a hard pencil, transferring an outline
to the can.

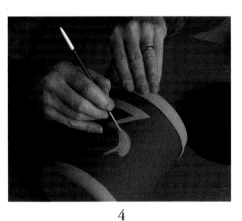

4

Fill in the main body of the "3"
in corn yellow.

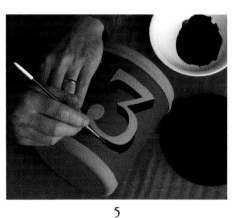

5

Fill in the shadow in black.

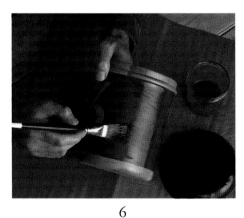

6

Varnish the can with shellac to give it
a warm glow.

7

Apply a coat of tinted varnish and then
give it a coat of clear satin varnish
to protect the surface.

Curtain-pole Hanging Display

The Victorian clothes airer made use of the warmth above the stove in the days before tumble dryers. These days they are seldom used for their original purpose; instead they are adorned with hooks that hold copper pans, baskets and other delights.

However, not all ceilings are suitable for a heavy airer, and some are not high enough for a hanging display of this sort. For the country look without the creaking timbers and bumped heads, try this attractive, painted curtain pole.

The wooden curtain poles used here can be bought from any hardware store.

MATERIALS

*curtain pole, plus turned finials
(not brackets)
2 large "eye" bolts for ceiling beam
medium-grade sandpaper
emulsion paint in green, red and
cream*

*household paintbrushes
clear varnish tinted with raw
umber acrylic paint
2 equal lengths of chain
cup hooks and butcher's hooks
for displays*

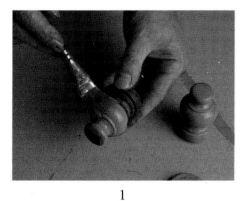

1

Using the pole as a measuring guide, position and screw into the ceiling or beam the two "eye" bolts. These must be very sturdy and firmly fixed. Sand down the pole and finials, and then paint the finials green.

2

Paint the pole red. When the pole is dry, paint the cream stripes 2½ in from the ends.

3

Sand the paint in places to give an aged look. Fit the finials on the ends of the pole. Apply a coat of tinted varnish. Attach the lengths of chain to the "eye" bolts. Screw in two cup hooks to the pole in the correct position to line up with the bolts. Attach the butcher's hooks for hanging your decorations, hang up the pole and add your display.

Embroidered Valance

*In France, valances such as this one are often pinned up above windows
that do not need curtains, but that would otherwise be too plain.*

The embroidery is simply made from a
few basic stitches and is quite suitable
for a beginner to attempt. Gingham
curtains provide a simple contrast
without detracting from the embroidered
pattern, but you could make plain
curtains and embroider them with the
same designs – if you have time and have
fallen under the embroidery spell!

MATERIALS

*tracing paper
dressmaker's transfer paper or
carbon pencil
1 yd plain cotton fabric, cut into
2 strips 8 in deep
needle and embroidery thread
in 4 colors
scissors
curtain wire*

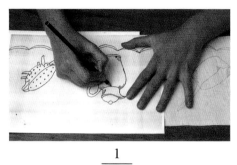

1

Enlarge the patterns from the template
section to approximately 4 in. Use transfer
paper or carbon pencil to transfer the patterns
on to the fabric.

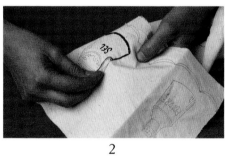

2

Depending on your knowledge and level of
skill, embroider each of the designs.
A simple chain-stitch can be used, but
cross-stitch, stem-stitch, back-stitch and
French knots will add variety.

3

Use satin-stitch to make the scalloped edge.
Carefully trim the edge. Sew a seam along
the top edge and thread a length of curtain
wire through it. Gather to fit the window.

Trompe-l'œil Dhurrie

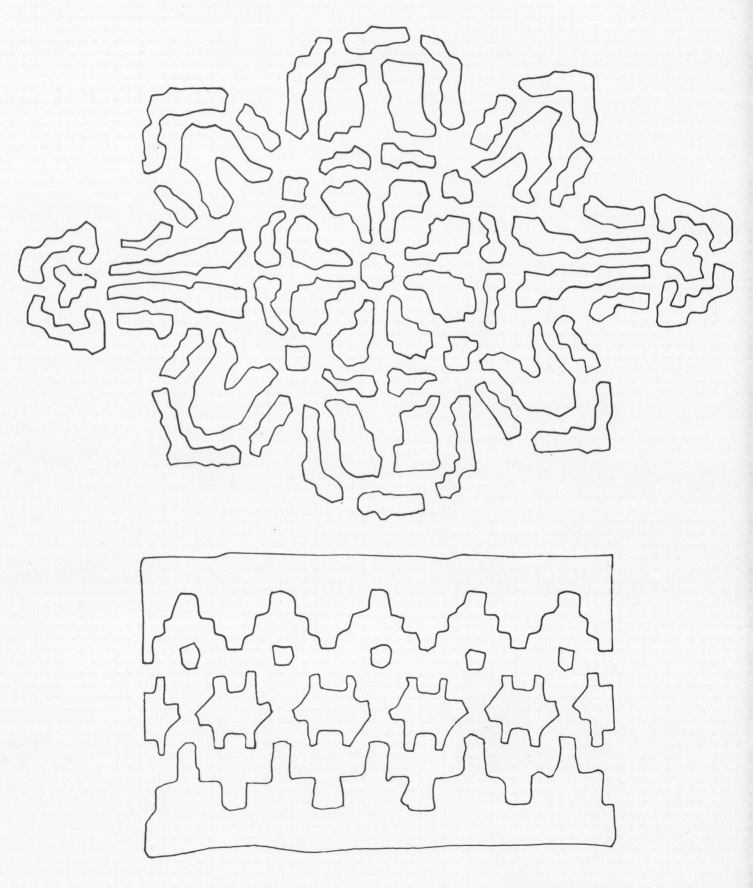

Canvas Floor Cloth

Stenciled Border

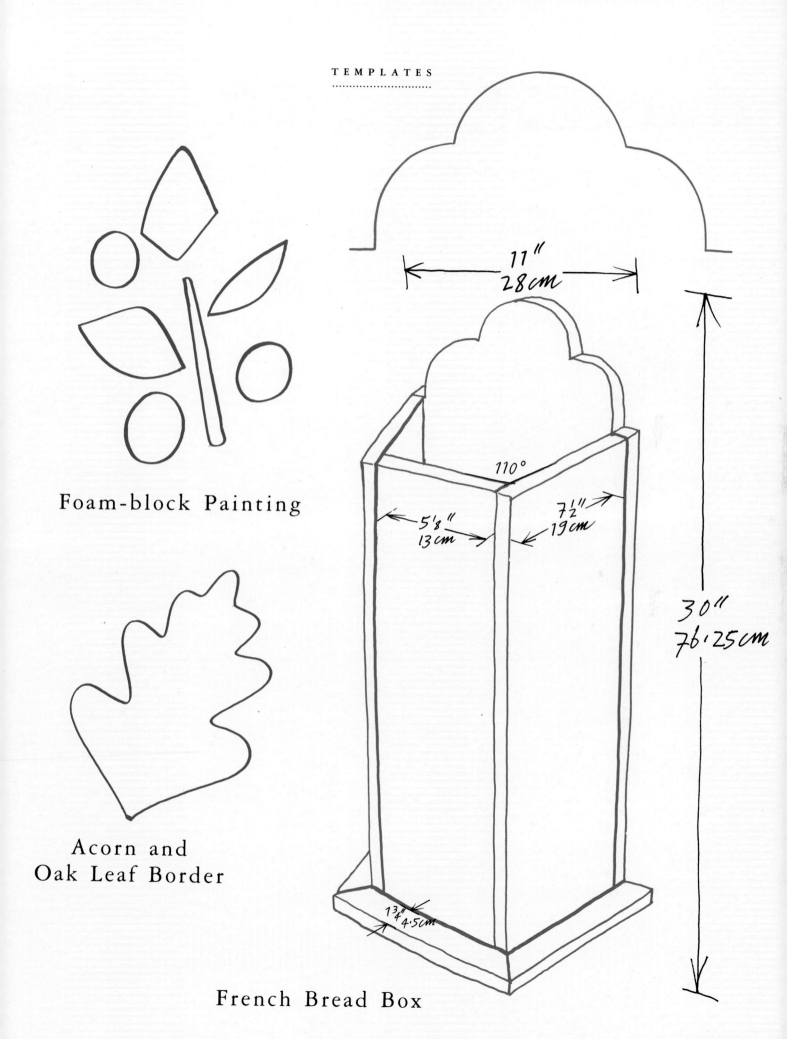

Foam-block Painting

Acorn and
Oak Leaf Border

11"
28cm

110°

5⅛"
13cm

7½"
19cm

30"
76·25cm

1¾"
4·5cm

French Bread Box

Painted Chest

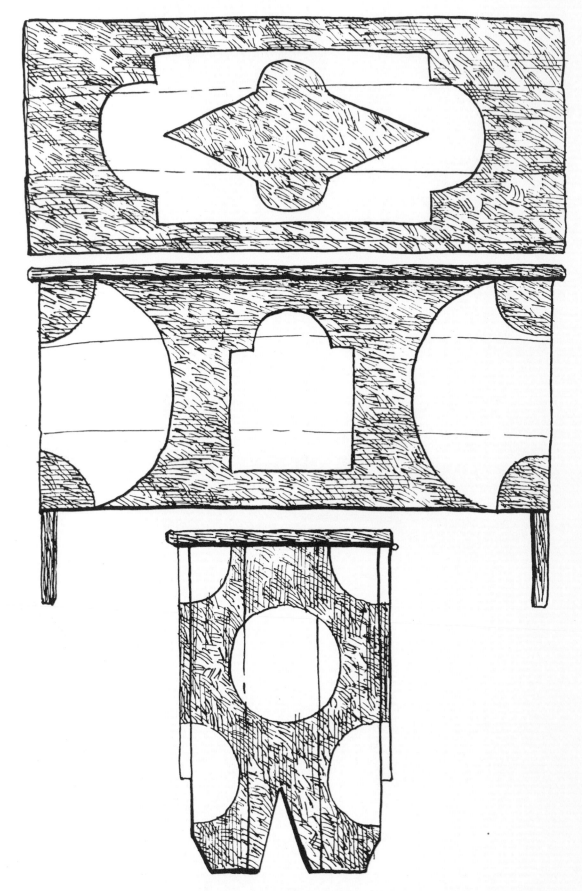

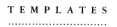

Rabbit Dummy Board

Shelf Bracket and Dummy Board Stand

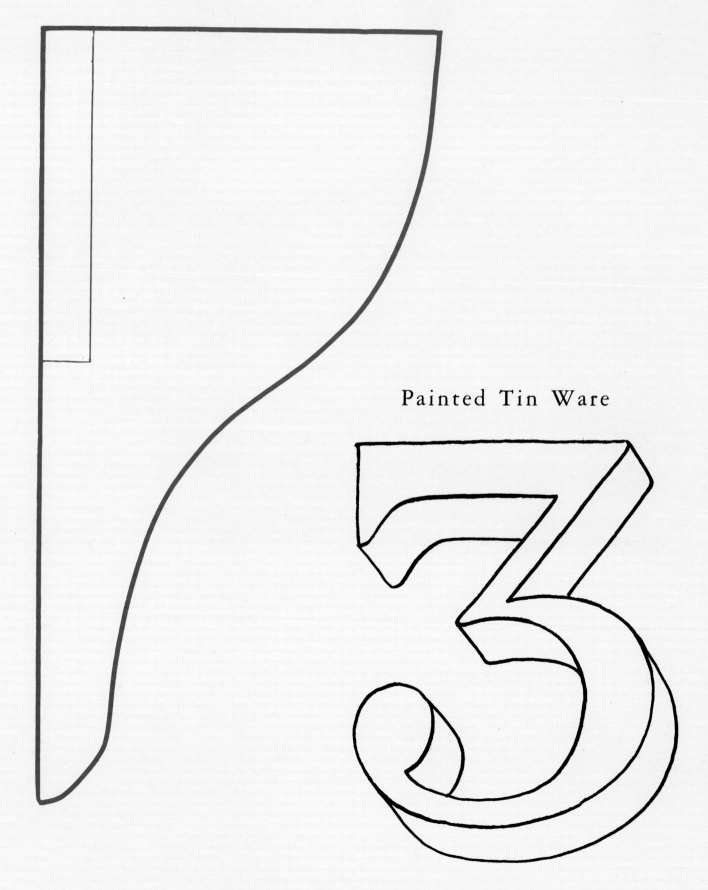

Painted Tin Ware

Embroidered Valance

COUNTRY
Crafts and
Flowers

TESSA EVELEGH

Fresh from the Fields

....

Nothing captures the mood of the season better than bringing a little of the outdoors inside. Harvest flowers, herbs and greenery from your own garden, the fields, and even the market place; gather together a few simple containers to put your treasures in; and then enjoy the abundance of seasonal colors, textures and aromas.

Fresh Herb Wreath

Gather together a basketful of sweet fresh herbs and make them into an aromatic wreath, to hang in the kitchen or to use as a decorative garland for a celebration. If you choose the fleshier herbs — which hold their moisture — and spray the wreath well, it should last for a couple of days; after this you may wish to dismantle it and dry the individual bunches of herbs.

MATERIALS

florist's wire
scissors
fresh sage
fresh or dried lavender
fresh parsley
hot glue gun and glue sticks
wreath base, about 12 in diameter
fresh chives
raffia

1

Using the florist's wire, wire all the herbs except the chives into generous bunches.

2

Using the glue gun, attach fix two bunches of sage to the wreath base, stems pointing inwards.

3

Next, attach enough lavender bunches side by side to cover the width of the wreath base, hiding the sage stems. Attach bunches of parsley to cover the lavender stems in the same way.

4

Work around the wreath base in this way until it is generously covered by the herbs.

5

Wire the chives into four generous bunches and trim the cut ends straight. Form each pair into a cross and bind it with raffia. Wire the crosses into position.

6

Tie raffia around the wreath at intervals. Make a raffia hanging-loop, thread this on to a generous bundle of raffia at the center top, and tie the ends of the bundle into a bow to finish.

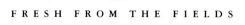
Provençal Herb Hanging

Fix bunches of fresh herbs to a thick braided rope, add tiny terra cotta pots to give the design structure and then fill it in with garlic and colorful chilies to make a spicy, herbal gift full of Provençal flavor, for anyone who loves to cook.

MATERIALS

hank of seagrass string
scissors
garden twine
florist's wire
fresh sage
fresh thyme
fresh oregano
2 small flowerpots
6 florist's stub wires
2 garlic heads
hot glue gun and glue sticks (optional)
large dried red chilies

1

Cut six lengths of seagrass string about three times as long as the desired finished length of the hanging. Take two lengths, fold them in half and place them under a length of garden twine. Pass the cut ends over the twine and through the loop of the fold, thereby knotting the seagrass on to the garden twine. Repeat twice with the remaining four seagrass lengths. Divide the seagrass into three bundles of four lengths and braid them to form the base of the herb hanging.

2

Finish the end of the braid by binding it with a separate piece of seagrass string.

3

Using florist's wire, bind the herbs into small bundles and tie each one with garden twine. Use this to tie them to the braided base.

4

Wire the flowerpots by passing two stub wires through the central hole and twisting the ends together.

5

Wire the pots to the base by passing a stub wire through the wires on the pots, passing it through the braid, and then twisting the ends together.

6

Tie garden string around the garlic heads and tie these to the base. Wire or glue the chilies into position, and fill the pots with more chilies.

Fresh-flower Fruit Bowl

Make the prettiest summer fruit bowl by arranging trailing flowers and foliage through a wire basket, topping it with chicken wire and a pretty plate, and then piling on the fresh fruit. This is a delightful touch for outdoor entertaining.

MATERIALS

*jelly jar
wire basket
fuchsia flowers or
similar trailing blooms
garden shears
chickenwire to fit the diameter
of the basket
attractive plate to fit the
diameter of the basket
selection of colorful fruit*

1

Fill the jelly jar with water and place it in the center of the basket.

2

Trim the flower stems with garden shears and arrange them all round the basket by threading the stems through the wire and into the jar of water. Continue until the flowers and foliage provide a delicate curtain of color around the basket.

3

Cut the chickenwire to fit over the basket and fix it by bending it around the rim. Place a plate on this chickenwire, and then fill the plate with colorful summer fruits.

Vegetable Centerpiece

The flower shop is not the only source of material for centerpieces — the vegetable stand provides great pickings, too. Here, a still life of ornamental cabbages — complemented by a simple cut open red cabbage and some artichokes — makes a flamboyant focal point for the table. The theme is carried through by adding an ornamental cabbage leaf to the silverware bundle at each setting.

MATERIALS

dyed raffia
painted wooden basket
2 ornamental cabbages in pots
lichen moss
1 set of silverware and napkin
per person
baby food jar
painted trug
red cabbage, halved
globe artichokes

1

Tie a bow of dyed raffia around the handle of the wooden basket. Remove several perfect cabbage leaves and place the cabbages in their pots in the basket.

2

Cover the tops of the pots with silvery-gray lichen moss.

3

Tie up each silverware bundle with a napkin and an ornamental cabbage leaf. Finish the arrangement by putting a few more leaves into a baby food jar and tying dyed raffia around it. Fill a garden trug with the red cabbage halves and the globe artichokes.

Candle Centerpiece

Even the humblest materials can be put together to make an elegant centerpiece. The garden shed has been raided for this one, which is made from a terra cotta flowerpot and chickenwire. Fill it up with red berries, ivies and white roses for a rich, Christmassy look; or substitute seasonal flowers and foliage at any other time of the year.

MATERIALS

7 in flowerpot
about 39 in chickenwire
knife
florist's foam ball to fit
the diameter of the pot

beeswax candle
tree ivy
white roses
berries
variegated trailing ivy

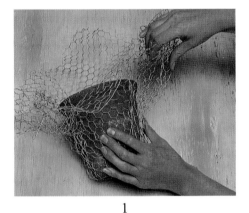

1

Place the pot in the center of a large square of chickenwire. Bring the chickenwire up around the pot and bend it into position.

2

Cut the florist's foam ball in half and soak one half. The other half isn't needed.

3

Place the foam in the pot, cut-side up so you have a flat surface. Position the candle in the center of the pot.

4

Arrange glossy tree-ivy leaves all around the candle, to provide a lush green base.

5

Add a white rose as a focal point, and bunches of red berries among the ivy.

6

Add more white roses, and intersperse trailing variegated ivy among the tree ivy, to give a lighter feel.

Wild at Heart

Often, the simplest arrangements are the most appealing. Here, flowers are arranged very simply in little glass jars wound around with blue twine and carefully grouped to make a delightful still life.

MATERIALS

blue twine	scabious
2 jam jars	anemones
garden shears	glass plate

1

Wrap the blue twine around the jars and tie securely. Fill the jars with water.

2

Fill one jar with scabious and another with anemones, cutting the stems to the right lengths as you go.

3

Fill the plate with water.

4

Cut one of the flower stems very short and allow the bloom to float in the plate. This is a delightful solution for any heads of flowers that have broken off during transit.

Advent Candle Ring

An Advent candle ring makes a pretty Christmas centerpiece. This one — decorated with glossy green tree ivy, Cape gooseberries, dried citrus fruit slices and bundles of cinnamon sticks — is a delight to the eye, while giving off a rich seasonal aroma.

MATERIALS

florist's foam
knife
florist's ring basket
4 church candles
moss
dried orange slices
florist's stub wires
garden shears
cinnamon sticks
golden twine
tree ivy
Cape gooseberries

1

Soak the florist's foam and cut it to fit the ring basket.

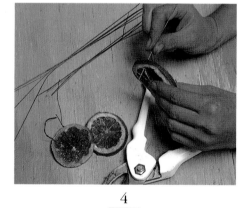

2

Position the candles in the foam.

3

Cover the florist's foam with moss, pushing it well down at the sides of the basket.

4

Wire the orange slices by passing a stub wire through the center, and then twisting the ends together at the outside edge. Wire the cinnamon sticks into bundles, then tie them with golden twine and then pass a wire through the string.

5

Wire the tree-ivy leaves into bundles.

6

Position the ivy leaves into the ring. Decorate by fixing in the orange slices and cinnamon sticks and placing the Cape gooseberries on top of the candle ring at intervals.

FRESH FROM THE FIELDS

Autumn Fruitfulness

The sheer beauty of autumn produce makes it difficult to resist. It's too good to be left in the pantry. Gather together all the softly bloomed purple fruits and pile them into a rich seasonal display for a side table or centerpiece.

MATERIALS

*metal urn
filling material, such as
bubble-wrap, newspaper or
florist's foam
several varieties of plums
black grapes
hydrangea heads
globe artichokes
blueberries*

1

So as not to waste a huge amount of fruit, fill the bottom of the urn with bubble-wrap, newspaper or florist's foam.

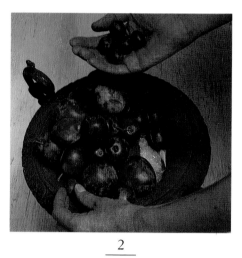

2

Arrange as many different varieties of plums as you can find on the filling, saving a few for the final decoration.

3

Add a large bunch of black grapes, draping them over the rim of the urn. Finish the arrangement with hydrangea heads, artichokes, scattered plums and blueberries.

....

Autumn Gold

The golds of autumn can be gathered into a fabulous display, using even the humblest of containers. Here, the dahlias have simply been put into a Mason jar and given a seasonal necklace of hazelnuts.

MATERIALS

hazelnuts
seagrass string
garden shears
dahlias
Mason jar
pumpkins
branches of pyracantha
with berries

<u>1</u>

Tie the hazelnuts on to the seagrass string
to make a necklace .

<u>2</u>

Cut about ½ in off the end of each dahlia
stem and place the stems in the Mason jar
filled with water.

<u>3</u>

Tie the hazelnut necklace around the jar.
Finish the arrangement with pumpkins
and pyracantha branches.

Springtime Garland

Garlands of fresh flowers make delightful decorations for any celebration.
This pretty little hanging of pansies and violas has a woodland feel that can be
recreated at any time, because these flowers are available in
most months of the year.

garden shears
chickenwire the desired length of
the garland and three times the
desired width
scissors
black plastic trash bag
about two pansy plants for every
6 in of garland
about six viola plants for every
6 in of garland
florist's stub wires
moss

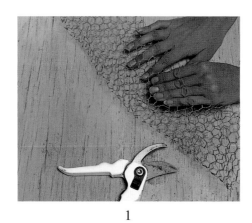

1

Using garden shears, cut the chickenwire to size and then form it into a flattened roll.

2

Cut the trash bag into squares large enough to cover the rootballs of the pansies and violas.

3

One by one, unpot each plant, gently remove any loose soil and place the rootball in the center of a square of trash bag.

4

Gather the plastic around the rootball and
fix it in place by winding stub wires loosely
round the top, leaving a short length free
to fix to the garland.

5

Fix the bagged-up plants to the garland
using the free end of wire.

6

Finish off by covering any visible plastic with
moss, fixing it with short lengths of florist's
stub wire bent hairpin style.

Summer Gift Basket

Fresh flowers are always a welcome gift — make them into something extra special by laying them in a basket with prettily packaged, home-made strawberry jam.

MATERIALS

jar of strawberry jam
pink paper
glue
paper strawberry print
scissors
glazed pink paper
raffia
wooden basket
colored paper
roses

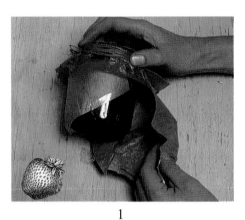

1

Make up a pretty presentation for the strawberry jam by wrapping the jar with pink paper and gluing on a paper strawberry print to fix the paper.

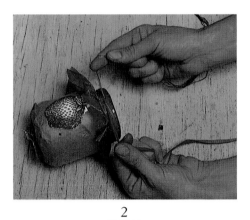

2

Make a top of glazed pink paper and a raffia tie. Line the basket with colored paper and fill it with a bunch of roses, tied with raffia, and the strawberry jam.

Christmas Gift Basket

Decorate a willow basket with gilded ivy leaves, and then pack it with seasonal goodies: a pot of variegated ivies and berries, decorative florist's pineapples, plus a few extra treats like beeswax candles and crystallized fruits.

MATERIALS

tree ivy
Treasure Gold®
willow basket
scissors
burlap
pot of variegated ivy with berries
presents

1

Gild the tree ivy by rubbing on Treasure Gold®, using your fingers. Decorate the rim of the basket with these gilded leaves.

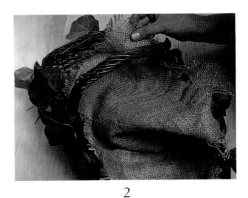

2

Cut a piece of burlap to size and fray the edges. Use it to line the basket. Add the pot of ivy, plus presents to fill the basket.

FRESH FROM THE FIELDS

Twig Heart Door Wreath

Welcome seasonal guests with a door wreath that's charming in its simplicity.
Just bend twigs into a heart shape and adorn the heart with variegated ivy,
berries and a Christmas rose, or substitute any pure white rose.

MATERIALS

garden shears
pliable branches, such as
buddleia, cut from the garden
florist's wire
seagrass string
variegated trailing ivy
red berries
tree ivy
Treasure Gold®
(optional)
white rose
golden twine

1

Using garden shears, cut six lengths of pliable branches about 28 in long. Wire three together at one end. Repeat with the other three. Cross the two bundles over at the wired end.

2

Wire the bunches together in the crossed-over position.

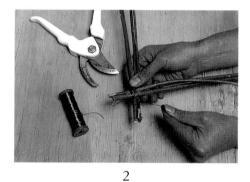

3

Holding the crossed, wired ends with one hand, ease the long end round and down very gently, so the branches don't snap. Repeat with the other side, to form a heart shape. Wire the bottom end of the heart.

4

Bind the wiring with seagrass string at top and bottom and make a hanging loop at the top.

5

Entwine trailing ivy around the heart shape.

6

Add berries. Make a posy of tree-ivy leaves (if you like, gild them using Treasure Gold®) and a white rose. Tie the posy with golden twine. Wire the posy in position at the top of the heart.

110

Tied Posy

Flowers are at their most appealing when kept simple. Just gather together some garden cuttings and arrange them in a pretty posy that the recipient can simply unwrap and put right into a vase, without any arranging.

MATERIALS

garden shears	*scabious*
roses	*brown paper*
eucalyptus	*ribbon*

1

Using garden shears, cut each flower stem to approximately 6 in long.

2

Gather the flowers together, surrounding each rose with some feathery eucalyptus, and then adding the scabious.

3

Wrap the posy with paper and tie it with a pretty ribbon bow.

Tussie Mussie

Traditionally, tussie mussies were bouquets of concentrically arranged aromatic herbs that were carried around as a personal perfume. This one combines the blue-greens of sage and thyme with the soft blues of lavender and scabious flowers.

MATERIALS

6 scabious
fresh thyme
fresh lavender
fresh sage
dyed raffia

1

Encircle the scabious blooms
with fresh thyme.

2

Arrange a circle of lavender around this,
making sure the piece keeps its circular shape.

3

Add a circle of sage, then tie with a
generous bundle of dyed raffia.

Easter Display

Colored eggs immediately transform springtime flowers into an Easter display. Simplicity is the secret: just gather together an abundance of flowers and add a few eggs, carefully laid on to moss to evoke the idea of a nest.

MATERIALS

*hard-boiled eggs
food dye if you want to eat the
eggs, or fabric dye if they are
purely for decoration
one jam jar for each color
vinegar
salt
garden shears
tulips or any spring flowers
vase
moss
plate*

1

First wash the eggs, and then prepare the dye. Do this by emptying half a small bottle of food dye or half a packet of fabric dye into a jam jar, and then pouring on 1¼ cups of hot water.

2

Add 2 tbsp vinegar and 1 tbsp salt. Lower an egg into the jam jar of dye and leave it for a few minutes. Check the color regularly.

3

When the egg has reached the desired color, lift it out and repeat with the rest. You will find that the more eggs you dye, the weaker the solution will become, so you'll have to leave the eggs in longer to achieve the same effect. Cut about ½ in off the end of each flower stem with garden shears, and then place them in a vase. Complete the arrangement by arranging the eggs on the moss on a plate.

Everlasting
Treats

....

*Nature offers many exquisite textures and colors
that have natural everlasting qualities – or
that can be encouraged to have them – so scour the
countryside, dried-flower suppliers, and even
your own pantry for flowers, leaves, grasses
and dried whole spices; collect richly textured
strings, raffias and twines; and then transform
them into delightfully lasting natural gifts.*

Lavender Basket

A basket decorated with bunches of dried lavender makes an exquisitely pretty aromatic linen store. It could also be kept on the kitchen counter, filled with freshly laundered dish towels ready on hand when you need them.

MATERIALS

dried lavender (2 bunches for the handle plus about 1 bunch for every 4 in of basket rim)

*florist's wire
scissors
willow basket*

*hot glue gun and glue sticks
blue paper-ribbon
blue twine*

1

Wire up enough small bundles of about six lavender heads to cover the rim of the basket generously. Arrange the heads so they are staggered to give fuller cover. Trim the stalks short.

2

Wire up the remaining lavender into 12 larger bunches of about 12 lavender heads for the handles, leaving the stalks long.

3

Form a star of three of the larger bunches and wire them together. Repeat with the other nine so you have four largish star-shaped bunches of lavender.

4

Fix the small bunches to the rim of the basket, using either wire or hot glue in a glue gun. Start at one end and work towards the handle. Use the bunches generously so they overlap each other to cover the width of the rim.

5

Once the rim is fully covered, glue on individual heads of lavender to cover any spaces, ugly wires or stalks. Pay particular attention to the area near the handles, because you will have finished up with quite a few bare stalks there.

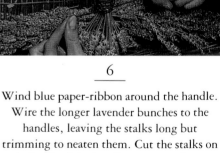

6

Wind blue paper-ribbon around the handle. Wire the longer lavender bunches to the handles, leaving the stalks long but trimming to neaten them. Cut the stalks on the inside of the handle shorter to fit the space. Bind the wired joints with blue twine.

E V E R L A S T I N G   T R E A T S
....

Heart of Wheat

Fashion a heart at harvest time, when wheat is plentiful, for a delightful decoration that would look good adorning a wall or a dresser at any time of the year. Despite its delicate feathery looks, this heart is quite robust and should last many years.

MATERIALS

*scissors
heavy-gauge garden wire
or similar
florist's tape
florist's wire
large bundle of wheat sheaves*

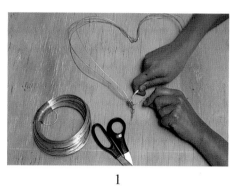

1

Cut three long lengths of heavy-gauge wire and bend them into a heart shape. Twist the ends together at the bottom.

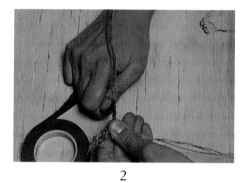

2

Use florist's tape to bind the wire heart shape.

3

Using florist's wire, make up enough small bundles of wheat sheaves to cover the wire heart shape densely. Leave a short length of wire at each end for fixing to the heart shape.

4

Starting at the bottom, tape the first bundle of wheat sheaves to the heart.

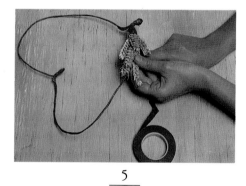

5

Place the second bundle further up the heart shape behind the first, and tape it in position. Continue until the whole heart is covered.

6

For the bottom, wire together about six bunches of wheat sheaves, twist the wires together and wire them to the heart, finishing off with florist's tape to neaten. This is what the back should look like by the time you've finished.

Flower Topiary

Dried flowers look fabulous when given the sculptural form of faux topiary.
These strawflowers and larkspur set into a tall cone make a stunning everlasting
display. Wrap the pot in a coordinating fabric to finish off the arrangement.

MATERIALS

small flowerpot
square of fabric to cover the pot
knife
small florist's dry foam cone
4 florist's stub wires
florist's dry foam cone,
about 7 in tall
scissors
bunch of dried blue larkspur
florist's wire, if necessary
bunch of dried
yellow strawflowers

1

Stand the pot in the center of the fabric and
tuck the corners into the pot. Tuck in any
other loose portions of fabric.

2

Cut down the small foam cone to fit the
inside of the pot. Position four stub wires
so they project above the foam. Use these
for attaching the top cone.

3

Snip the florets off the larkspur, leaving the
small stalks to push into the foam. Make four
rows of larkspur down the length of the cone
to quarter it; then fill in either side of these
rows to create broad blue bands. Many of the
florets' stalks will be strong enough to pierce
the foam. If not, wire the florets with
florist's wire. Finally, fill in the panels
with the strawflowers.

Leaf and Petal Decorations

Decorations are so much more appealing when made from all things natural.
These, made from preserved oak and beech leaves and dried hydrangea flowers,
are easy to do, and they make delightful tree or table decorations.

scissors
dried mop-head hydrangeas
(about two for every ball)
hot glue gun and glue sticks
florist's dry foam balls, about
3 in in diameter
glycerined beech leaves
glycerined or dyed, dried
oak leaves
Treasure Gold®

1

Snip the florets off the mop-head hydrangeas.
Put aside the florets that have the prettiest
coloring on the top side of the petals. Leave
a little stalk on these, but trim the stalks off
the rest. Carefully glue a floret top side
down on to a florist's ball.

2

Continue to glue the florets face downwards
until the ball is completely covered.

3

Put a tiny drop of glue on the back of each of
the petals of a reserved floret. Fix this,
top-side up, on to the ball – over the base
covering of petals. If you leave a little stalk
on the florets you set aside for the top layer,
this can be used to help attach it to the ball.
Let the glue work just where the petals touch
the ball, allowing them to curl naturally at
the edges to provide texture. Continue until
the ball is covered. To make the leaf balls,
first gild the beech leaves with Treasure
Gold®. Stick the beech and oak leaves over
the ball, overlapping them slightly to
cover the foam.

Hydrangea Pot

Dried materials can be used to make the simplest, yet most exquisite, gifts.
Here's an easy but effective idea, using a single hydrangea head.

MATERIALS

glue
dyed, dried oak leaf
small flowerpot
dyed raffia
scissors
dried mop-head hydrangea

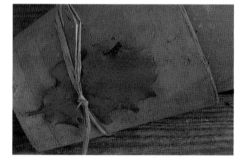

1

Use a drop of glue to attach the leaf to the pot,
and then tie it on with raffia. Secure the raffia
tie at the back with another drop of glue.

2

Cut the hydrangea stalk short enough so that
the head rests on the pot. Place the head
in the pot.

Spice Pots

For a cook, make a cornucopia of culinary flavorings by putting different dried
herbs and spices into terra cotta pots and packing the pots in a wire basket.

MATERIALS

cinnamon sticks
dried bay leaves
garlic
dried red chilies
small flowerpots
wire basket
wire
raffia

1

Place the herbs and spices in the pots and
place the pots in the basket.

2

Bend a piece of wire into a heart shape and
bind it with raffia. Leave a long end free.
When complete, the end can be used to tie
the heart to the basket.

Leafy Pictures

Delicate skeletonized leaves come in such breathtakingly exquisite forms that they deserve to be shown off. Mount them on handmade papers and frame them to make simple yet stunning natural collages.

MATERIALS

wooden picture frame
sandpaper
paint
paintbrush
backing paper
pencil
scissors
skeletonized leaf
Treasure Gold®
hot glue gun and glue sticks
mounting paper

1
___

Take the frame apart and sand it down to provide a base before painting. A translucent colorwash has been used for painting here, but any paint will do.

2
___

Allow the paint to dry, then sand the paint back so you're left with a wooden frame with shading in the moldings, plus a veil of color on the surface.

3
___

Use the back of the frame as a template for the backing paper. Draw around it with a pencil to form a cutting line.

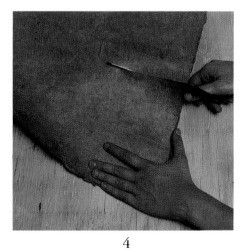

4
___

Cut the backing paper out.

5

Prepare the leaf by rubbing with Treasure Gold®. This does take a little time as the gilt has to be well worked in.

6

Stick the backing paper on the frame back, glue the mounting paper in the center and attach the leaf on to that. Here, the leaf is centered with the stalk breaking the edge of the mounting paper. Finally, put the frame back together.

EVERLASTING TREATS

Natural Christmas Decorations

Raid the pantry and scrap box, add garden clippings plus dried fruit slices, and you have the ingredients for delightful Christmas decorations that can be individually hung or tied on to the tree, or strung on to twine to make a garland.

MATERIALS

florist's stub wires
bundles of twigs
Treasure Gold®
dried bay leaves
dried pear slices
fabric scraps
dried apple slices
dried orange slices
small rubber bands
cinnamon sticks
gold twine
beeswax candle ends

1

Wire together bundles of twigs, and then gild them by rubbing in Treasure Gold®.

2

Make up the fruit bundles. Make a small loop at one end of a florist's stub wire. Thread on some dried bay leaves, and then a dried pear, passing the wire through the rind at the top and bottom. Make a hook at the top.

3

Tie a scrap of colored fabric to the bottom loop and a scrap of green (synthetic chiffon is shown) at the top, to look like leaves. Make the apple slice bundles by threading on first the thick apple slices, and then the bay leaves.

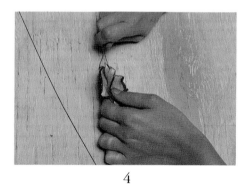

4

Wire up pairs of thinner sliced apples by passing a wire through the center and twisting the wires together at the top. Wire up the orange slices in the same way.

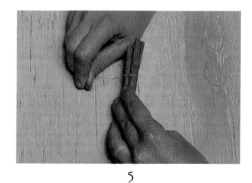

5

Use small rubber bands to make up bundles of cinnamon sticks.

6

Either hang each decoration directly on the tree or make up a garland to hang on the tree or at the window. Here, they have been strung together using gold twine. The beeswax candle-ends are simply knotted in at intervals.

Everlasting Christmas Tree

This delightful little tree, made from dyed, preserved oak leaves and decorated with tiny gilded cones, would make an enchanting Christmas decoration. Make several and then group them to make a centerpiece, or place one at each setting.

MATERIALS

*garden shears
bunch of dyed, dried oak leaves
florist's wire
small pine cones
Treasure Gold®
knife
flowerpot, 7 in tall
small florist's dry foam cone
4 florist's stub wires
florist's dry foam cone,
about 7 in tall*

1

Cut the leaves off the branches and trim the stalks. Wire up bunches of about four leaves, making some bunches with small leaves, some with medium-sized leaves and others with large leaves. Sort the bunches into piles.

3

Prepare the pot as with the flower topiary on page 122 by cutting the smaller foam cone to fit the pot, adding stub-wire stakes and positioning the larger cone on to this. Attach the leaves to the cone, starting at the top with the bunches of small leaves, and working down through the medium and large leaves to make a realistic shape. Add the gilded cones to finish.

2

Insert wires into the bottom end of each fir cone and twist the ends together. Gild each cone by rubbing on Treasure Gold®.

Fruited Tree

Glycerined leaves make a perfect foundation for any dried topiary. You can buy them in branches, ready glycerined for use, or glycerine your own garden prunings. Here, they have been wired into bunches for a fabulous, full look.

MATERIALS

*garden shears
3 branches of glycerined
beech leaves
florist's stub wires
dried pear slices
florist's dry foam ball, about
5 in diameter
flowerpot, 7 in tall*

1

Cut the leaves off the branches and trim the stalks short. Wire up small bunches of four or six beech leaves and twist the ends of the wires together.

2

Pass a stub wire through the top of each pear slice and twist the ends together.

3

Completely cover the portion of the ball that will show above the pot with beech leaves.

4

Add the pear slices and put the ball into the pot.

Spice Topiary

Fashion a delightfully aromatic, culinary topiary from cloves and star anise, pot it in terra cotta decorated with cinnamon sticks and top with a cinnamon-stick cross. Sticking all the cloves into the oasis is both easy to do and wonderfully therapeutic.

MATERIALS

small rose pot
knife
cinnamon sticks
hot glue gun and glue sticks
florist's dry foam cone,
about 9 in tall
small florist's dry foam cone
florist's stub wires
large pack of star anise
cloves

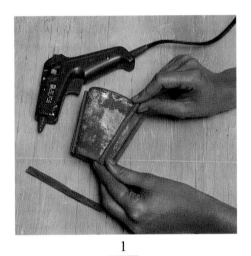

1

Prepare the pot by cutting the cinnamon sticks to the length of the pot and gluing them in position.

2

Trim off the top of the larger cone and rework it into a pleasing shape that is stubbier than the original. Cut the smaller cone to fit inside the pot.

3

Put four stub wires upright into the pot so they project above the foam. Use these to stake the sculpted cone on top of the foam-filled pot.

4

Sort out all the complete star anise from the pack, plus any that are almost complete — you'll need about 20 in all. Wire these up by passing a wire over the front in one direction, and another wire over the front in another direction to make a cross of wires. Twist the wires together at the back and trim to about ½ in.

E V E R L A S T I N G   T R E A T S
....

5

Start by arranging the star anise in rows down the cone – about three each side to quarter the cone. Put two vertically between each line. Next, just fill the whole remaining area of cone with cloves, packing them tightly so none of the foam shows through.

6

Glue two short pieces of cinnamon stick into a cross. Wire this up, and use it to decorate the top.

Dried-flower Pot

Dried flowers always look their best when the blooms are massed and the stalks not too prominent. Here's a charming treatment: roses and lavender tucked into a tiny terra cotta pot, and then tied around with raffia.

MATERIALS

knife
small florist's dry foam cone
small rose pot
dried rosebuds
scissors or garden shears
dried lavender
dyed raffia
hot glue gun and glue sticks

1
___

Trim the foam to fit the pot. Place the rosebuds around the edge of the pot.

2
___

Cut the lavender stalks to about ½ in and use them to fill the center of the arrangement. Tie a dyed raffia bow around the pot and secure it at the back with a drop of glue.

Everlasting Basket

Hydrangeas look fabulous dried, providing a flamboyant display that can simply be massed into a basket. They're also about the easiest flowers to dry at home. Just put the cut flowers in about ½ in of water and leave them. The flowers will take up the water and then gradually dry out.

MATERIALS

knife
florist's dry foam
painted wooden basket
dried mop-head hydrangeas
dried artichokes
ribbon

1

Cut the florist's foam to fit and fill the basket, and then arrange the hydrangeas to cover the top of the basket.

2

Add the dried artichoke at one end for texture.

3

Tie a ribbon to the handle of the basket to finish.

Dried-herb Wreath

A dried-herb wreath based on lavender makes a wonderful, textural, aromatic wall hanging. This one also incorporates artemesia, tarragon, lovage and large French lavender seedheads.

MATERIALS

scissors
florist's wire
dried lavender
dried artemesia
dried lovage
dried tarragon
hot glue gun and glue sticks
small wreath base
French lavender seedheads

1

Wire all the dried herbs and flowers, except the French lavender seedheads, into small bunches.

2

Using a glue gun, fix a bunch of lavender to the wreath base.

3

Next, glue a bunch of artemesia to the wreath base.

4

Work around the base, adding a bunch of lovage.

5

Continue all round the wreath, interspersing the different bunches of herbs to cover it completely, using the tarragon to add a feathery look.

6

Finally, for structure, add the individual French lavender seedheads.

Love and Kisses Collage

*This witty natural collage is made from tropical seedheads and cinnamon sticks
mounted on cheesecloth. Even the frame has been decorated with giant
cinnamon sticks, glued over a simple wooden one.*

MATERIALS

*wooden picture frame
brown backing paper
scissors
linen cheesecloth
hot glue gun and glue sticks
knife
small cinnamon sticks
florist's wire
heart-shaped or any other large
tropical seedheads
4 huge cinnamon sticks*

1

Take the glass out of the picture frame and
stick the backing paper to the hardboard
backing. Cut the linen cheesecloth to size,
and fray the edges. Put drops of glue all
around the edge of the muslin and then
stick it to the backing.

2

Glue six short lengths of cinnamon into
three crosses, and then wire them up to form
a delicate metallic cross joint.

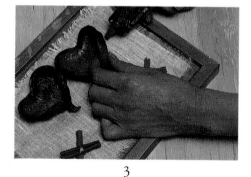

3

Glue the heart-shaped seedheads to the top
of the picture; glue the cinnamon kisses
to the bottom.

4

Finish by making a cinnamon-stick frame.
Cut two huge cinnamon sticks to the same
length as the frame and two to the same as
the width. First glue a stick to the top of the
frame, and then one to the bottom. Next,
glue the side ones to these.

Decorative Dried Artichokes

The exquisite pinky shades at the base of some dried artichokes are too beautiful to be covered up by containers. Show them off by balancing the artichokes across pots covered in linen cheesecloth to make wonderful natural decorations.

MATERIALS

small flowerpot
square of linen cheesecloth
dyed raffia
dried artichokes with
a pinky-purple hue

1

Place the pot in the center of the linen cheesecloth and tuck the fabric corners into the pot.

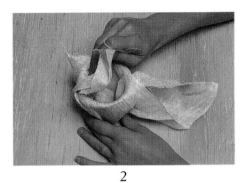

2

Tuck in any other loose ends, and then tie everything in place with raffia. Make an arrangement by balancing the artichokes on the pot to show off the depth of color on the undersides.

Spicy Pomander

Pomanders were originally nature's own air fresheners. The traditional orange pomanders are fairly tricky to do, because the critical drying process can so easily go wrong, leading to moldy oranges. This one, made of cloves and cardamom pods, offers none of those problems, and makes a refreshing change in soft muted colors.

MATERIALS

cloves
florist's dry foam ball,
about 3 in diameter
hot glue gun and glue sticks
green cardamom pods
raffia
florist's stub wire

1

Start by making a single line of cloves all around the circumference of the ball. Make another one in the other direction, so you have divided the ball into quarters.

2

Make a line of cloves on both sides of the original lines to make broad bands of cloves quartering the ball.

3

Starting at the top of the first quarter, glue cardamom pods over the foam, methodically working in rows to create a neat effect. Repeat on the other three quarters.

4

Tie a bow in the center of a length of raffia. Pass a stub wire through the knot and twist the ends together.

EVERLASTING TREATS

5

Attach the bow to the top of the ball
using the stub wire.

6

Join the two loose ends in a knot
for hanging the pomander.

Country Gifts

....

What can bring more pleasure than gifts inspired by country traditions? They have a quality that acknowledges the seasons and withstands the test of time. Gather together all the natural materials you can find — shells, papers, natural fabrics, wire, and even chickenwire — and turn them into something very special.

Sleep Pillow

Many people still swear by sleep pillows, which are traditionally filled with chamomile and hops. Since hops are related to the cannabis plant, they induce a feeling of sleepy well-being, while chamomile helps you to relax. Either buy ready-prepared sleep mix, or make up your own with chamomile, lemon verbena and a few hops. Stitch a pillow filled with these relaxing herbs to keep on your bed, and look forward to a good night's sleep.

MATERIALS

*linen muslin, 80 × 8 in
(this can be made up of two
or more shorter lengths)
pins, needle and thread
scissors
pure cotton fabric, 20 × 10 in
herbal sleep mix
39 in antique lace
39 in ribbon, ½ in wide
4 pearl buttons*

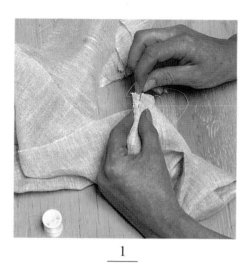

1

Prepare the linen muslin border by stitching together enough lengths to make up 80 in. With right sides facing, stitch the ends together to form a ring. Trim the seam. Fold the ring in half lengthwise with wrong sides facing and run a line of gathering stitches close to the raw edges.

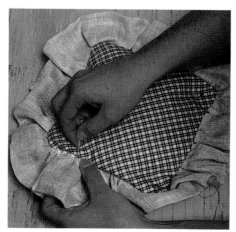

2

Cut two pieces of cotton fabric into 10 in squares. Pull up the gathering threads of the muslin to fit the cushion edge. Pin it to the right side of one square, with raw edges facing outwards, matching the raw edges and easing the gathers evenly round the cushion. Put the second square on top and pin the corners. Stitch the seams, leaving a gap for stuffing. Trim the seams.

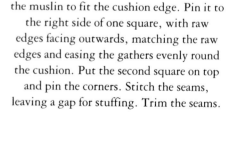

3

Turn the cushion rightside out and fill it with herbal sleep mix. Stitch the gap to enclose the border.

4

Using tiny stitches, sew the lace to the
cushion about 1 in away from the border.

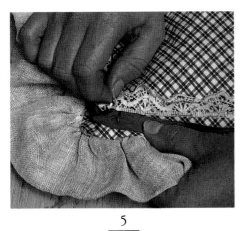

5

Stitch the ribbon close to the lace, making
a neat diagonal fold at the corners.

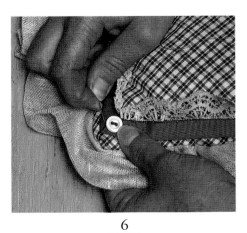

6

Finish by sewing a tiny pearl button
to each corner.

Herb Pot-holder

Protect tabletops from hot pots and pans with an aromatic mat, filled with cinnamon, cloves and bay leaves. The heat of the pot immediately releases the fragrance of its contents, kept evenly distributed with mattress-style ties.

MATERIALS

scissors
mattress ticking, at least
25 × 22 in
pins, needle and thread

*spice mix to fill, e.g. dried bay
leaves, cloves, cinnamon sticks
heavyduty upholstery needle
cotton string*

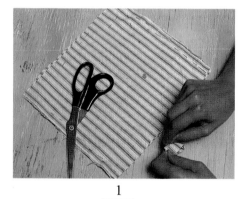

1

First make the hanger by cutting a strip of ticking 2 × 12 in. With right sides facing, fold this in half lengthwise. Stitch the long side, leaving the ends open. Trim the seam. Turn right side out and press. Fold in half to form a loop. Cut two rectangles from the fabric measuring about 25 × 20 in.

2

Place the cushion pieces on a flat surface, right sides facing, and then slip the hanging loop between the layers, with the raw edges pointing out towards a corner.

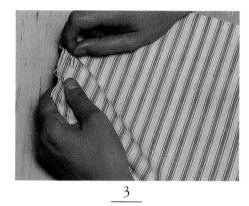

3

Pin and stitch the cushion pieces together, leaving about 3 in open. Trim the seams. Turn right side out.

4

Fill the cushion with the spices.

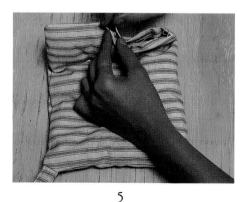

5

Slip-stitch to close the opening.

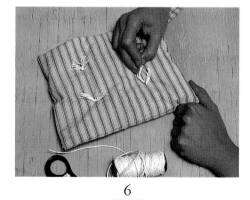

6

Using a heavyduty upholstery needle threaded with cotton string, make a stitch about a third in from two sides of the cushion, clearing the spices inside the mat away from the area as you go. Untwist the strands of the string for a more feathery look. Repeat with three other ties to give a mattress effect. Make a simple knot in each to secure the ties.

Lavender Sachets

Use fabric scraps to appliqué simple motifs on to charming checked fabrics, and then stitch them into sachets to fill with lavender and use as drawer-fresheners. Inspired by traditional folk art, these have universal appeal.

MATERIALS

scissors
fabric scraps
paper for templates
pins, needle and thread
stranded embroidery thread in
different colors
loose dried lavender
button

1

Cut two pieces of fabric into squares about 6 in. If you are using a checked or striped fabric, it is a good idea to let the design dictate the exact size. Scale up the template and use it as a pattern to cut bird and wing shapes from contrasting fabrics. Pin and baste the bird shape to the right side of one square.

2

Neatly slip-stitch the bird shape to the sachet front, turning in the edges as you go. Repeat with the wing shape.

3

Using three strands of embroidery thread in a contrasting color, make neat running stitches around the bird and its wing.

4

Make long stitches on the tail and wing to indicate feathers, graduating them into a pleasing shape. Sew on the button eye.

5

With right sides facing, stitch the front and back of the sachet together, leaving a 2 in gap. Trim the seams. Turn it right side out and press. Fill with dried lavender, and then slip-stitch to close the gap.

Lacy Lavender Heart

Evocative of the Victorian era, this exquisitely pretty heart-shaped lavender bag is made from simple, creamy muslin, and trimmed with antique lace and satin ribbon. The chiffon ribbon at the top is tied into a loop for hanging on coat hangers with favorite garments.

MATERIALS

paper for template *scissors* *silky muslin, about* *24 × 8 in*	*pins, needle and stranded* *embroidery thread* *pearl button* *loose dried lavender*	*20 in antique lace* *20 in very narrow* *satin ribbon* *20 in medium ribbon*

1

Make a heart-shaped paper template about 6 in high and use this as a pattern. Cut four heart shapes from muslin. Tack the hearts together in pairs so each heart is a double thickness of muslin.

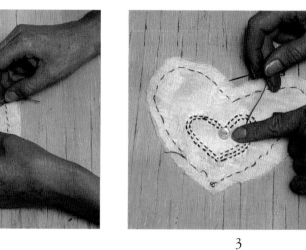

2

Cut a smaller heart shape from muslin. Carefully stitch this to the center front of one of the larger heart shapes, using two strands of embroidery thread and a running stitch. Make another row of running stitches inside this.

3

Sew the button to the top of the smaller heart.

4

Stitch a third row of running stitches inside the other two. Allow the edges of the smaller heart to fray. With right sides facing, stitch all around the edge of the two large double-thickness muslin heart shapes, leaving a gap of 2 in. Trim the seams, snip into the seam at the 'V' of the heart and snip off the bottom point within the seam allowance. Turn the heart right-side out. Fill it with lavender and slip-stitch to close the gap. Don't despair if the heart looks pretty miserable and misshapen at this stage!

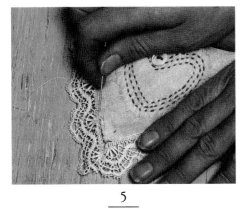

__5__

Carefully slip-stitch the lace around the edge
of the heart.

__6__

Stitch the satin ribbon over the lower edge
of the lace.

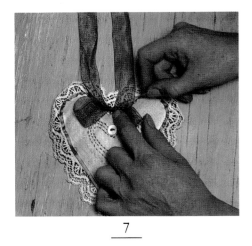

__7__

Finish with a ribbon bow, arranging it so the
long tails are upwards as these can then be
joined to form a loop for hanging on
coat hangers in the wardrobe.

Herb Bath-sachet

Enjoy a traditional herbal bath by filling a fine muslin bag with relaxing herbs, tying it to the faucet and letting the hot water run through. This drawstring design means it can be reused time after time if you keep refilling it with new herbs. Chamomile and hops are relaxing; basil, bay, mint, lemon balm and sage are invigorating.

MATERIALS

silky muslin, about 12 × 16 in pins, needle and thread   *scissors fabric scraps, for casing 39 in narrow ribbon*   *safety pin herbal bath-mix or any combination of dried herbs*

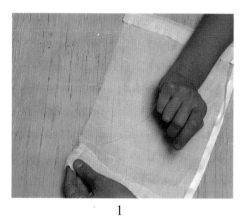

1

With right sides facing, fold over about 2 in of the silky muslin at both short ends, pin and stitch each side. Trim the seams. Turn right-side out.

2

Turn in and hem the raw edges of the folded-over ends.

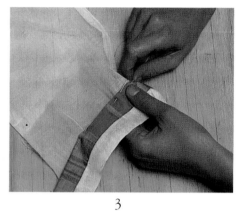

3

Cut two strips of cotton fabric about 1 in wide and as long as the width of the muslin, with about ¼ in extra for turnings all round. Iron a hem along both long edges. Turn in and hem the ends, then pin one casing on the right side of the muslin so the bottom edge of the casing lines up with the hem line. Neatly stitch the casing in place along both long seams. Repeat with the other casing.

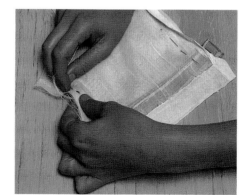

4

With right sides together, fold the muslin in half so the casings line up. Stitch the side seams from the bottom edge of the casing to the bottom edge of the bag. Trim the seams.

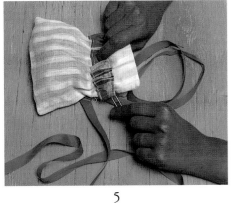

5

Cut the ribbon in half, attach a safety pin to one end and use this to thread the ribbon through the casing so both ends finish up at the same side. Remove the safety pin.

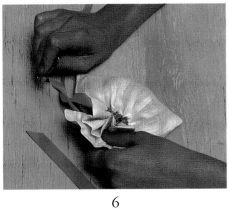

6

Attach the safety pin to one end of the other piece of ribbon and thread it through the casing in the other direction so the ends finish up at the other side. Fill with herbs ready for use.

Shell Pot

Decorate a flowerpot with shells and some old netting, and then use it to hold plants, pencils, paintbrushes, strings, ribbon, or any paraphernalia that needs to be kept in check. It's a pretty and inexpensive way to make a very special container.

MATERIALS

small net bag
flowerpot, 7 in tall
scissors
hot glue gun and glue sticks
thick string
small cowrie shells
cockle shells
starfish or similar central motif

1

Slip the net bag over the flowerpot and trim the top edge. Secure it by gluing on a length of string.

2

Using a glue gun, position a row of cowrie shells along the top edge.

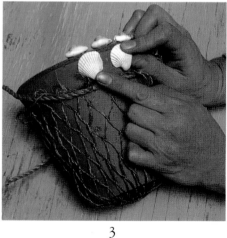

3

Glue cockle shells around the rim; position the starfish and four cockle shells in the front.

Shell Box

A simple cardboard box takes on a South Seas feel when decorated with half-cowries. Available from craft shops, their flattened bottoms make them easy to stick to surfaces. Here, some have also been strung together to make a toggle for fastening.

MATERIALS

*hot glue gun and glue sticks
raffia
small cardboard box
half-cowrie shells
upholstery needle*

___1___

Glue a loop of raffia from the bottom of the box, up the back and along the top.

___2___

Tie half-cowries into a bunch on a length of raffia, tying each one in separately. Leave a short length of raffia free. Pierce the front of the box with an upholstery needle and thread the raffia through. Knot it on the inside.

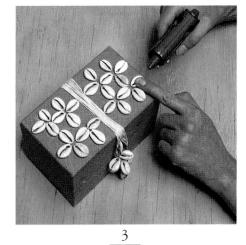

___3___

Glue on a pattern of half-cowries to decorate the outside of the box.

Shell Candle Centerpiece

An old flowerpot, scallop shells salvaged from the fish market and smaller shells picked up from the beach make up a fabulous centerpiece. Put a candle in the center or fill it with dried fruits or flowers.

MATERIALS

hot glue gun and glue sticks
8 curved scallop shells
flowerpot, 7 in tall
bag of cockle shells
4 flat scallop shells
newspaper, florist's foam or
other packing material
saucer
candle
raffia

1

Generously apply hot glue to the inside lower edge of a large curved scallop shell. Hold it in place on the rim of the pot for a few seconds until it is firmly stuck. Continue sticking shells to the top of the pot, arranging them so they overlap slightly, until the whole of the rim has been covered.

2

In the same way, glue a cockle shell where two scallops join. Continue all around the pot.

3

Place another row of cockles at the joins of the first row. Glue flat scallop shells face upwards to the bottom of the pot, first at the front, then at the back, and then the two sides, to ensure the pot stands straight.

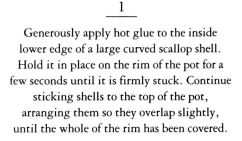
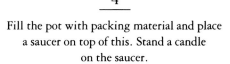

4

Fill the pot with packing material and place a saucer on top of this. Stand a candle on the saucer.

5

Tie raffia around the pot where it joins the stand.

6

Decorate the stand with a few more cockles, if you like. Stand a few more curved scallop shells inside the original row to create a fuller, more petalled shape.

Shell Mirror

*The subtle rose-pinks of ordinary scallop shells, picked up from the fish market,
make for an easy, eye-catching mirror frame. Here, four large shells
have been used at the corners with smaller ones filling in the sides.*

MATERIALS

*sandpaper
mirror in wooden frame
paint
paintbrush
4 large flat scallop shells
hot glue gun and glue sticks
10 small flat scallop shells
seagrass string
2 metal eyelets*

1

Sand down and paint the mirror frame with
the color of your choice.

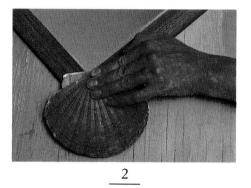

2

Position the large scallop shells at the corners
of the mirror, using the hot glue.

3

In the same way, glue three of the smaller
scallop shells to each side of the mirror.

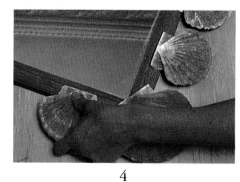

4

Attach two of the smaller scallop shells to the
top of the mirror and two to the bottom.

5

Braid three lengths of seagrass string
to make a hanger.

6

Screw metal eyelets into each side of the
frame at the back, and tie the hanger
on to these.

Chickenwire Heart

*The garden shed provided the materials for this heart. Two shapes are simply cut
from chickenwire and joined to give a more three-dimensional effect; then
they are decorated with string. The heart is lovely hung on the wall inside;
if it is decorated with a heavyduty garden string it could also be hung outside.*

*newspaper for template
scissors
chickenwire
wire cutters or garden shears
paper string or any sturdy string*

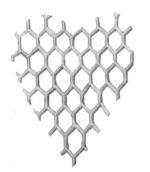

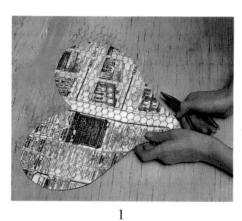

1

Cut a heart template about 14 in long from
newspaper. Use this as a pattern to cut two
heart shapes from chickenwire.

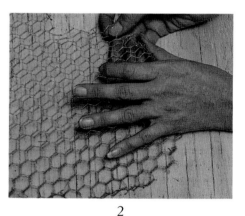

2

Place one chickenwire heart on top of the
other, and bend in the edges sharply all
round to join the shapes.

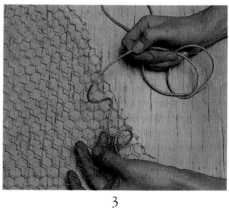

3

Thread sturdy string all around the edges
to finish, leaving two long ends free at the
center. Thread a separate piece of string at
the center top, and tie the ends together to
make a hanging loop.

COUNTRY GIFTS

·····························

Raffia Heart

This charming heart starts life, somewhat inauspiciously, as a coat hanger.
With the hook cut off, the hanger is simply bent to shape, ready to be wrapped
with raffia. A similar tiny heart, made from heavy-gauge reel wire, is hung in
the center to finish it off.

MATERIALS

wire coat hanger
wire cutters or garden shears
raffia
heavy-gauge wire

1

Bend the coat hanger into a heart shape
and cut off the hook.

2

Starting at the bottom of the heart and
leaving a free length of raffia, wind raffia
around the heart to meet in the middle again.
Tie the two ends together.

3

Make a smaller heart from wire and bind it
with raffia. Use raffia to tie the smaller heart
so that it hangs inside the larger one.
Tie a hanging loop on to the larger heart.

161

Natural Stationery

Add your own personal style to a simple brown paper file folder or notebook, by making closures from anything on hand. Here, an auger shell and a bundle of cinnamon sticks make elegant toggles, with loops made from twine and raffia.

MATERIALS

*plain buff stationery folder
or notebook
auger shell or cinnamon sticks
upholstery needle
raffia or twine
hot glue gun and glue sticks
2 small squares of brown paper*

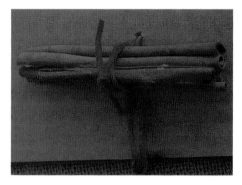

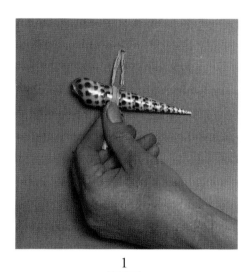

1

Work out the best position on the file folder or notebook for the shell or cinnamon sticks toggle. Using an upholstery needle, pierce a hole in this position. Pass a loop of raffia through this to the front. Pass a short piece of raffia through this loop.

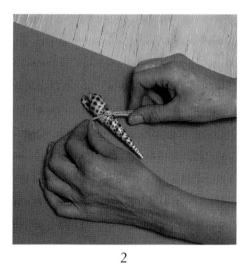

2

Tie the short piece of raffia around the shell or cinnamon stick. Secure it with a drop of glue.

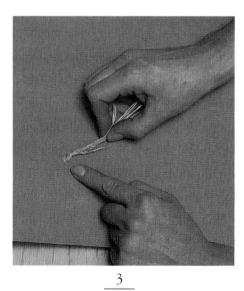

3

Open the folder or notebook. Tie a knot in the raffia close to the cover. Trim the ends.

4

On the back cover, make a hole in a similar position to the one on the front cover. Thread a loop of raffia through this. Test the length by bringing it around the front and experimenting with buttoning and unbuttoning the shell or sticks, bearing in mind you will need extra slack to allow for knotting the loop in place. Make a knot in the raffia on the inside.

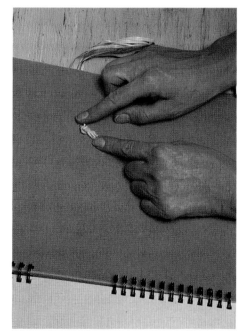

162

COUNTRY GIFTS

....

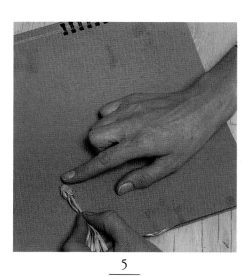

5

Close the folder or book and make another knot close to the cover on the outside so the loop is fixed firmly. Test the loop for size again, and if necessary, undo the knots and re-knot them in the right place.

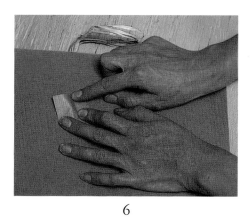

6

Cover the knots on the insides of the covers by gluing on the small squares of brown paper to avoid damage to the adjoining pages. This is also useful if you are using material for the loop that could stain the pages, such as colored twine or a leather thong.

163

Filigree Leaf Wrap

Even the most basic brown wrapping paper can take on a very special look. Use a gilded skeletonized leaf and gold twine in combination with brown paper: coarser string would give a more robust look.

MATERIALS

*Treasure Gold®
large skeletonized leaf
brown paper
sticky tape
gold twine
hot glue gun and glue sticks,
if necessary*

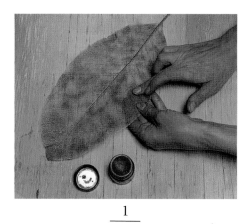

1

Rub Treasure Gold® into the skeletonized leaf.

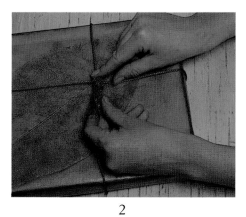

2

Wrap the parcel in the brown paper and rub Treasure Gold® on to the corners. Tie the parcel with gold twine, bringing the two ends together and tying a knot. Fray the ends to create a tassle effect. Slip the leaf under the twine, securing it with glue at each end if necessary.

Fruit and Foliage Gift Wraps

Here, gilded brown parcel paper provides a fitting background for a decoration of leaves and dried fruit slices.

MATERIALS

*brown paper
sticky tape
Treasure Gold®
seagrass string
hot glue gun and glue sticks
dried fruit slices
preserved leaves*

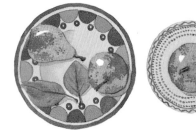

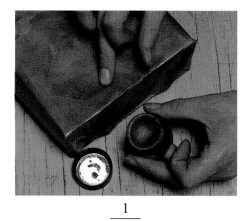

1

Wrap the package with brown paper and rub in Treasure Gold®, paying special attention to the corners.

2

Tie the parcel with seagrass string, and then glue a different dried fruit or leaf to each quarter.

Tissue Rosette Gift Wrap

Tissue papers make a fabulous foundation for any gift-wrapping; they come in a glorious array of colors, and they softly take to any shape.

M A T E R I A L S

tissue paper in 2 shades
coordinating twine

1

Place a cylindrical gift in the center of two squares of tissue, one laid on top of the other. Gather the tissue up and tie it with twine.

2

Gently open out the rosette at the top.

Lavender Tissue Gift Wrap

Bunches of lavender add a real country touch to tissue gift wrap, and become part of the gift.

M A T E R I A L S

dried lavender
twine
tissue paper in 2 shades
sticky tape
glue

1

Make two bunches of lavender and tie them with twine to form a cross.

2

Wrap the package in the darker toned tissue paper, and then wrap it with the paler tissue, cut to form an envelope. Glue the lavender to the front of the package.

Bath-lotion Bottle

Recycle a glass bottle containing homemade lotion and decorate it with corrugated cardboard in gem-like colors for a real impact.

scissors
colored corrugated cardboard
flower water bottle
hot glue gun and glue sticks
colored raffia

1

Cut the corrugated cardboard to size, and then glue in position around the bottle. Tie with raffia.

2

Make a matching label from corrugated cardboard, and tie it on using raffia.

Bath-lotion Jar

Decorate a jar of lotion to complement the bottle, using brilliantly colored fine corrugated cardboard. Royal blue and emerald green make a rich combination that could be used for both men and women.

scissors
colored corrugated cardboard
baby food jar
hot glue gun and glue sticks
twine

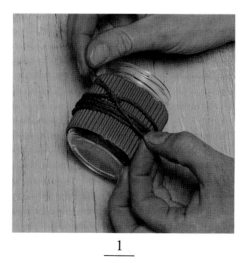

1

Cut the corrugated cardboard to size, and then glue in place around the jar. Tie the twine around the jar.

2

Cut a piece of corrugated cardboard to fit the top of the lid and glue it in place. Glue twine to cover the side of the lid.

COUNTRY
Cooking

LIZ TRIGG

Spring Recipes

....

*Spring brings the first of the year's tender young
vegetables, and there are plenty of tempting recipes
to make the most of seasonal produce. Treat yourself
to a zesty lemon cake or an Easter bread studded
with fruit and spices, for an Easter breakfast.*

Spring Roasted Chicken with Fresh Herbs and Garlic

A smaller chicken or four squabs can also be roasted in this way.

INGREDIENTS

*4½ lb free-range chicken or
4 small squabs
finely grated rind and
juice of 1 lemon
1 garlic clove, crushed
2 tbsp olive oil
2 fresh thyme sprigs
2 fresh sage sprigs
6 tbsp unsalted butter,
softened
salt and freshly ground
black pepper*

Serves 4

1

Season the chicken or squabs well.
Mix the lemon rind and juice, garlic and
olive oil together and pour them over the
chicken. Leave to marinate for at least
2 hours in a non-metallic dish.
When the chicken has marinated preheat
the oven to 450°F.

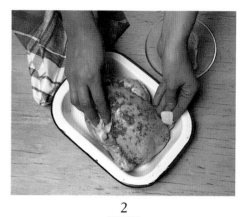

2

Place the herbs in the cavity of the bird and
smear the butter over the skin. Season well.
Roast the chicken for 10 minutes, then turn
the oven down to 375°F. Baste the chicken
well, and then roast for a further 1 hour
30 minutes, until the juices run clear when
the thigh is pierced with a skewer. Leave to
rest for 15 minutes before carving.

Lemon and Rosemary Lamb Chops

*Spring lamb is delicious with the fresh flavor of lemon. Garnish with sprigs of
fresh rosemary — the aroma is irresistible.*

INGREDIENTS

*12 lamb chops
3 tbsp olive oil
2 large rosemary sprigs
juice of 1 lemon
3 garlic cloves, sliced
salt and freshly ground
black pepper*

Serves 4

1

Trim the excess fat from the chops.
Mix the oil, rosemary, lemon juice and
garlic together and season well.
Preheat the broiler.

2

Pour over the chops in a shallow dish and
marinate for 30 minutes. Remove from the
marinade, and blot the excess with kitchen
paper and broil for 10 minutes on each side.

Carrot and Cilantro Soufflés

Use tender young carrots for this light-as-air dish.

INGREDIENTS

1 lb carrots
2 tbsp fresh chopped
cilantro
4 eggs, separated
salt and freshly ground
black pepper

Serves 4

<u>1</u>

Peel the carrots.

<u>2</u>

Cook in boiling salted water for 20 minutes
or until tender. Drain, and process until
smooth in a food processor.

<u>3</u>

Preheat the oven to 400°F. Season the
puréed carrots well, and stir in the chopped
cilantro.

<u>4</u>

Fold the egg yolks into the carrot mixture.

<u>5</u>

In a separate bowl, whisk the egg whites
until stiff.

<u>6</u>

Fold the egg whites into the carrot mixture
and pour into four greased ramekins. Bake
for about 20 minutes or until risen
and golden. Serve immediately.

SPRING RECIPES

....

Leeks with Ham and Cheese Sauce

A tasty lunch or supper dish: use a strong cheese for best results.

INGREDIENTS

4 leeks
4 slices ham

For the sauce
2 tbsp unsalted butter
1 tbsp all-purpose flour
1 1/4 cups milk
1/2 tsp French mustard
4 oz Cheddar cheese, grated
salt and freshly ground
black pepper

Serves 4

1

Preheat the oven to 375°F. Trim the leeks to 1 in of the white and cook in salted water for about 20 minutes until soft. Drain thoroughly. Wrap the leeks in the ham slices.

2

To make the sauce, melt the butter in a saucepan. Add the flour and cook for a few minutes. Remove from the heat and gradually add the milk, whisking well with each addition. Return to the heat and whisk until the sauce thickens. Stir in the mustard and 3 oz of the cheese and season well. Lay the leeks in a shallow ovenproof dish and pour the sauce over. Scatter the extra cheese on top and bake for 20 minutes.

Baked Eggs with Heavy Cream and Chives

This is a rich dish best served with Melba toast: it's very easy and quick to make.

INGREDIENTS

1 tbsp unsalted butter,
softened
4 tbsp heavy cream
1 tbsp chopped fresh chives
4 eggs
2 oz Gruyère cheese,
finely grated
salt and freshly ground
black pepper

Serves 2

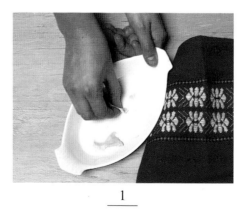

1

Preheat the oven to 350°F. Grease two individual gratin dishes. Mix the cream with the chives, and season with salt and pepper.

2

Break the eggs into each dish and top with the cream mixture. Sprinkle the cheese around the edges of the dishes and bake in the oven for 15–20 minutes. When cooked, brown the tops under the broiler for a minute.

Lemon Drizzle Cake

You can also make this recipe using a large orange instead of the lemons; either way, it makes a zesty treat for afternoon tea.

INGREDIENTS

finely grated rind of 2 lemons
³⁄₄ cup superfine sugar
1 cup unsalted butter, softened
4 eggs
2 cups self-rising flour
1 tsp baking powder
¹⁄₄ tsp salt
shredded rind of 1 lemon, and 1 tsp granulated sugar to decorate

For the syrup
juice of 1 lemon
³⁄₄ cup superfine sugar

Serves 6

1

Preheat the oven to 325°F. Grease a 2 lb loaf pan or 7–8 in round cake pan and line it with wax paper or baking parchment. Mix the lemon rind and superfine sugar together.

2

Cream the butter with the lemon and sugar mixture. Add the eggs and mix until smooth. Sift the flour, baking powder and salt into a bowl and fold a third at a time into the mixture. Turn the batter into the pan, smooth the top and bake for 1¹⁄₂ hours or until golden brown and springy to the touch.

3

To make the syrup, slowly heat the juice with the sugar and dissolve it gently. Make several slashes in the top of the cake and pour the syrup over. Sprinkle the shredded lemon rind and 1 tsp granulated sugar on top and leave to cool.

Whole Wheat Bread

Homemade bread creates one of the most evocative smells in country cooking.
Eat this on the day you bake it, to enjoy the superb fresh taste.

INGREDIENTS

¾ oz fresh yeast
1 ¼ cups lukewarm milk
1 tsp superfine sugar
1 ½ cups whole wheat flour,
sifted
2 cups all-purpose white flour,
sifted
1 tsp salt
4 tbsp butter, chilled and cubed
1 egg, lightly beaten
2 tbsp mixed seeds

Makes 4 round loaves or
2 long loaves

1

Gently dissolve the yeast with a little of the milk and the sugar to make a paste. Place both the flours plus any bran from the sifter and the salt in a large warmed mixing bowl. Rub in the butter until the mixture resembles bread crumbs.

2

Add the yeast mixture, remaining milk and egg and mix into a fairly soft dough. Knead on a floured board for 15 minutes. Lightly grease the mixing bowl and put the dough back in the bowl, covering it with a piece of greased plastic wrap. Let rise until double in size in a warm place (this should take at least an hour).

3

Punch the dough down and knead it for a further 10 minutes. Preheat the oven to 400°F. To make round loaves, divide the dough into four pieces and shape them into flattish rounds. Place them on a floured baking sheet and let rise for a further 15 minutes. Sprinkle the loaves with the mixed seeds. Bake for about 20 minutes until golden and firm.

NOTE

For pan-shaped loaves, put the punched-down dough into two greased loaf pans instead. Let rise for a further 45 minutes and then bake for about 45 minutes, until the loaf sounds hollow when turned out of the pan and knocked on the base.

Easter Braid

Serve this delicious bread sliced with butter and jam.
It is also very good toasted on the day after you made it.

INGREDIENTS

⅞ cup milk
2 eggs, lightly beaten
6 tbsp superfine sugar
4 cups all-purpose flour
½ tsp salt
2 tsp ground allspice
6 tbsp butter
¾ oz fresh yeast

1¼ cups currants
¼ cup candied mixed citrus
peel, chopped.
a little sweetened milk, to glaze
1½ tbsp candied cherries,
chopped
1 tbsp angelica, chopped

Serves 8

1

Warm the milk to lukewarm, add two-thirds
of it to the eggs and mix in the sugar.

2

Sift the flour, salt and allspice together.
Rub in the butter. Make a well in the center
of the flour, add the milk and yeast, adding
more milk as necessary to make a sticky dough.

3

Knead on a well-floured surface and then
knead in the currants and mixed peel,
reserving 1 tbsp for the topping. Put the
dough in a lightly greased bowl and cover
it with a damp dish towel. Let rise until
double its size. Preheat the oven to 425°F.

4

Turn the dough out on to a floured surface
and knead again for 2–3 minutes. Divide the
dough into three even pieces. Roll each
piece into a sausage shape roughly
8 in long. Braid the three pieces together,
turning under and pinching each end. Place
on a floured baking sheet and let rise
for 15 minutes.

5

Brush the top with sweetened milk and
scatter with coarsely chopped cherries, strips
of angelica and the reserved peel. Bake in the
preheated oven for 45 minutes or until the
bread sounds hollow when tapped on the
bottom. Cool slightly on a wire rack.

Orange-blossom Mold

A fresh orange gelatin mold makes a delightful dessert: the natural fruit flavor combined with the smooth gelatin has a clean taste that is especially welcome after a rich main course. This is delicious served with thin, crisp cookies.

INGREDIENTS

5 tbsp superfine sugar
2/3 cup water
2 packets of gelatin
(about 1 oz)
2½ cups freshly squeezed
orange juice
2 tbsp orange-flower water

Serves 4–6

1

Place the superfine sugar and water in a small saucepan and gently heat to dissolve the sugar. Leave to cool.

2

Sprinkle the gelatin over ensuring it is completely dissolved in the water. Let stand until the gelatin has absorbed all the liquid and is solid.

3

Gently melt the gelatin over a bowl of simmering water until it becomes clear and transparent. Leave to cool. When the gelatin is cold, mix it with the orange juice and orange-flower water.

4

Wet a mold and pour in the gelatin. Chill in the refrigerator for at least 2 hours, or until set. Turn out to serve.

Rhubarb and Orange Crumble

The almonds give this crumble topping a nutty taste and crunchy texture.
This crumble is extra-delicious with home-made custard.

INGREDIENTS

2 lb rhubarb, cut in
2 in lengths
6 tbsp superfine sugar
finely grated rind and juice
of 2 oranges

1 cup all-purpose flour
½ cup unsalted butter,
chilled and cubed
6 tbsp demerara sugar
1¼ cups ground almonds

Serves 6

1

Preheat the oven to 350°F. Place the rhubarb
in a shallow ovenproof dish.

2

Sprinkle the superfine sugar over and add the
orange rind and juice.

3

Sift the flour into a mixing bowl and add the
butter. Rub the butter into the flour until
the mixture resembles bread crumbs.

4

Add the demerara sugar and ground almonds
and mix well.

5

Spoon the crumble mixture over the fruit to
cover it completely. Bake for 40 minutes,
until the top is browned and the fruit is
cooked. Serve warm.

Summer Recipes

························

*The warm, lazy days and long nights of summer
provide the perfect excuse for outdoor dining
with friends and family. Try Mediterranean quiche
or a glorious garden salad with nasturtium flowers.
Cooling treats include strawberry fool, or
homemade mint ice cream.*

Mackerel with Roasted Blueberries

Fresh blueberries burst with flavor when roasted, and their sharpness complements the rich flesh of mackerel very well.

INGREDIENTS

2 tsp all-purpose flour
4 small cooked, smoked mackerel
4 tbsp unsalted butter
juice of ½ lemon
salt and freshly ground
black pepper

For the roasted blueberries
1 lb blueberries
2 tbsp superfine sugar
1 tbsp unsalted butter
salt and freshly ground
black pepper

Serves 4

1

Preheat the oven to 400°F. Season the flour. Dip each fish fillet into the flour to coat it well.

2

Dot the butter on the fillets and bake in the oven for 20 minutes.

3

Place the blueberries, sugar, butter and seasoning in a separate small roasting pan and roast them, basting them occasionally, for 15 minutes. To serve, drizzle the lemon juice over the roasted mackerel, accompanied by the roasted blueberries.

Pan-fried Trout with Bacon

This dish can also be cooked under the broiler.

INGREDIENTS

1 tbsp all-purpose flour
4 trout, cleaned and gutted
3 oz lean bacon
4 tbsp butter
1 tbsp olive oil
juice of ½ lemon
salt and freshly ground
black pepper

Serves 4

1

Pat the trout dry with paper towels and
mix the flour and seasoning together.

2

Roll the trout in the seasoned flour mixture
and wrap tightly in the bacon. Heat a
heavy frying pan. Heat the butter and
oil in the pan and fry the trout for 5 minutes
on each side. Serve immediately, with the
lemon juice drizzled on top.

Mediterranean Quiche

The strong Mediterranean flavors of tomatoes, peppers and anchovies
beautifully complement the cheese pastry in this unusual quiche.

INGREDIENTS

For the pastry
2 cups all-purpose flour
pinch of salt
pinch of mustard
½ cup butter, chilled and
cubed
2 oz Gruyère cheese, grated

For the filling
2 oz can of anchovies in oil,
drained
¼ cup milk
2 tbsp French mustard
3 tbsp olive oil
2 large Spanish onions, peeled
and sliced
1 red bell pepper, seeded and
very finely sliced
3 egg yolks
1½ cups heavy cream
1 garlic clove, crushed
6 oz sharp Cheddar
cheese, grated
2 large tomatoes, thickly sliced
salt and freshly ground
black pepper
2 tbsp chopped fresh basil,
to garnish

Serves 12

1

First make the pastry. Place the flour, salt
and mustard in a food processor,
add the butter and process the mixture
until it resembles bread crumbs.

2

Add the cheese and process again briefly.
Add enough iced water to make a stiff
dough: it will be ready when the dough
forms a ball. Wrap with plastic wrap and
chill for 30 minutes.

3

Meanwhile, make the filling. Soak the
anchovies in the milk for 20 minutes.
Pour off the milk.

4

Roll out the chilled pastry and line a 9 in
loose-based quiche pan. Spread the mustard
over and chill for a further 15 minutes.

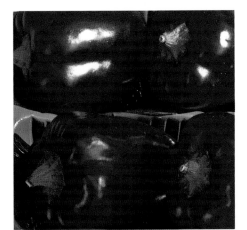

5

Preheat the oven to 400°F. Heat the oil in a
frying pan and cook the onions and red
pepper until soft. In a separate bowl, beat
the egg yolks, cream, garlic and Cheddar
cheese together; season well. Arrange the
tomatoes in a single layer in the pastry crust.
Top with the onion and pepper mixture
and the anchovy fillets. Pour the egg
mixture over. Bake for 30–35 minutes.
Sprinkle over the basil and serve.

New Potato Salad

Potatoes freshly dug up from the garden are the best. Always leave the skins on:
just wash the dirt away thoroughly. If you add the mayonnaise and other
ingredients when the potatoes are hot, the flavors will develop as the potatoes cool.

INGREDIENTS

2 lb baby new potatoes
2 green apples, cored and chopped
4 scallions, chopped
3 celery stalks, finely chopped
⅔ cup homemade or storebought
mayonnaise
salt and freshly ground
black pepper

Serves 6

1

Cook the potatoes in salted, boiling water
for about 20 minutes, or until they are
very tender.

2

Drain the potatoes well and immediately add
the remaining ingredients and stir until well
mixed. Let cool and serve cold.

Green Bean Salad

The secret of this recipe is to dress the beans while still hot.

INGREDIENTS

6 oz cherry tomatoes,
halved
1 tsp sugar
1 lb green beans, topped
and tailed
6 oz feta cheese, cubed
salt and freshly ground
black pepper

For the dressing
6 tbsp olive oil
3 tbsp white-wine vinegar
¼ tsp Dijon mustard
2 garlic cloves, crushed
salt and freshly ground
black pepper

Serves 6

1

Preheat the oven to 450°F. Put the cherry
tomatoes on a baking sheet and sprinkle the
sugar, salt and pepper over. Roast for 20
minutes, then let cool. Meanwhile, cook the
beans in boiling salted water for 10 minutes.

2

Make the dressing by whisking together the
oil, vinegar, mustard, garlic and seasoning.
Drain the beans and immediately pour the
vinaigrette over and mix well. When cool,
stir in the roasted tomatoes and the
feta cheese. Serve chilled.

Squash à la Greque

A traditional French-style dish that is usually made with mushrooms.
Make sure that you cook the baby squash until they are quite tender,
so they can fully absorb the delicious flavors of the marinade.

INGREDIENTS

6 oz pattypan squash
1 cup white wine
juice of 2 lemons
fresh thyme sprig
bay leaf
small bunch of fresh chervil,
coarsely chopped
¼ tsp coriander seeds, crushed
¼ tsp black peppercorns, crushed
5 tbsp olive oil

Serves 4

1

Blanch the pattypan squash in boiling
water for 3 minutes, and then refresh them
in cold water.

2

Place all the remaining ingredients in a pan,
add ⅔ cup of water and simmer for 10
minutes, covered. Add the patty pans and
cook for 10 minutes. Remove with a slotted
spoon when they are cooked and tender
to the bite.

3

Reduce the liquid by boiling hard for
10 minutes. Strain it and pour it over the
squashes. Leave until cool for the flavors to
be absorbed. Serve cold.

Garden Salad

You can use any fresh, edible flowers from your garden for this beautiful salad.

INGREDIENTS

1 Romaine lettuce
6 oz arugula
1 small frisée lettuce
fresh chervil and tarragon sprigs
1 tbsp chopped fresh chives
handful of mixed edible flower
heads, such as nasturtiums
or marigolds

For the dressing
3 tbsp olive oil
1 tbsp white-wine vinegar
½ tsp French mustard
1 garlic clove, crushed
pinch of sugar

Serves 4

1

Mix the Romaine, arugula and frisée leaves
and herbs together.

2

Make the dressing by whisking all the
ingredients together in a large bowl. Toss the
salad leaves in the bowl with the dressing,
add the flower heads and serve at once.

Country Strawberry Fool

*Make this delicious fool on the day you want to eat it, and chill it well,
for the best strawberry taste.*

INGREDIENTS

*1 ¼ cups milk
2 egg yolks
scant ½ cup superfine
sugar
few drops of vanilla extract
2 lb ripe strawberries, stemmed
and washed
juice of ½ lemon
1 ¼ cups heavy cream*

To decorate
*12 small strawberries
4 fresh mint sprigs*

Serves 4

1

First make the custard. Whisk 2 tbsp milk
with the egg yolks, 1 tbsp superfine sugar
and the vanilla extract.

2

Heat the remaining milk until it is just
below boiling point.

3

Stir the milk into the egg mixture. Rinse
the pan out and return the mixture to it.

4

Gently heat and stir until the custard
thickens enough to coat the back of a wooden
spoon. Lay a wet piece of wax paper on the
top of the custard and let it cool.

5

Purée the strawberries in a food processor or
blender with the lemon juice and the
remaining sugar.

6

Lightly whip the cream and fold in the fruit
purée and custard. Pour into glass dishes and
decorate with the whole strawberries and
sprigs of mint.

Mint Ice Cream

This ice cream is best served slightly softened, so take it out of the freezer 20 minutes before you want to serve it. For a special occasion, this looks spectacular served in an ice bowl.

8 egg yolks
6 tbsp superfine sugar
2½ cups light cream
1 vanilla bean
4 tbsp chopped fresh mint,
to garnish

Serves 8

1

Beat the egg yolks and sugar until they are pale and light using a hand-held electric beater or a balloon whisk. Transfer to a small saucepan.

2

In a separate saucepan, bring the cream to a boil with the vanilla bean.

3

Remove the vanilla bean and pour the hot cream on to the egg mixture, whisking briskly.

4

Continue whisking to ensure the eggs are mixed into the cream.

5

Gently heat the mixture until the custard thickens enough to coat the back of a wooden spoon. Let cool.

6

Stir in the mint and place in an ice-cream maker to churn, about 3–4 hours. If you don't have an ice-cream maker, freeze the ice cream until mushy and then whisk it well again, to break down the ice crystals. Freeze for another 3 hours until it is softly frozen and whisk again. Finally freeze until hard: at least 6 hours.

Mixed Berry Tart

The orange-flavored pastry is delicious with the fresh fruits of summer.
Serve this with some extra shreds of orange rind scattered on top.

INGREDIENTS

For the pastry
2 cups all-purpose flour
1/2 cup unsalted butter
finely grated rind of 1 orange,
plus extra to decorate

For the filling
1 1/4 cups crème fraîche
and 3/4 cup whipped cream
or 3/4 cup sour cream
finely grated rind of 1 lemon
2 tsp confectioner's sugar
1 1/2 lb mixed summer
berries

Serves 8

1

To make the pastry, put the flour and butter in a large bowl. Rub in the butter until the mixture resembles bread crumbs.

2

Add the orange rind and enough cold water to make a soft dough.

3

Roll into a ball and chill for at least 30 minutes. Roll out the pastry on a lightly floured surface.

4

Line a 9 in loose-based quiche pan with the pastry. Chill for 30 minutes. Preheat the oven to 400°F and place a baking sheet in the oven to heat up. Line the pan with wax paper and baking beans and bake blind on the baking sheet for 15 minutes. Remove the paper and beans and bake for 10 minutes more, until the pastry is golden. Allow to cool completely. To make the filling, whisk the crème fraîche, lemon rind and sugar together and pour into the pastry crust. Top with fruit, sprinkle with orange rind and serve sliced.

Autumn Recipes

....

*Reap the benefits of the autumn harvest with this
collection of recipes; wild mushroom tart,
thyme-roasted onions and duck and chestnut casserole
all make the most of autumn produce.
Warming desserts such as steamed ginger and
syrup pudding, or poached pears, are guaranteed to
keep away the autumn chill.*

Wild Mushroom Tart

*The flavor of wild mushrooms makes this tart really rich: use as wide a variety
of mushrooms as you can get.*

INGREDIENTS

For the pastry
2 cups all-purpose flour
4 tbsp Crisco
2 tsp lemon juice
about ²/₃ cup ice water
*¹/₂ cup butter, chilled and
cubed*
1 egg, beaten, to glaze

For the filling
10 tbsp butter
2 shallots, finely chopped
2 garlic cloves, crushed
*1 lb mixed wild mushrooms such as
porcini, oyster mushrooms, or
shiitake mushrooms, sliced*
3 tbsp chopped fresh parsley
2 tbsp heavy cream
*salt and freshly ground
black pepper*

Serves 6

1

To make the pastry, sift the flour and
¹/₂ tsp salt together into a large bowl.
Add the Crisco and rub into the mixture
until it resembles bread crumbs.

2

Add the lemon juice and enough ice water
to make a soft but not sticky dough.
Cover and chill for 20 minutes.

3

Roll the pastry out into a rectangle on a
lightly floured surface. Mark the dough into
three equal strips and arrange half the butter
cubes over two-thirds of the dough.

5

Chill the pastry for 20 minutes. Repeat the
process of marking into thirds, folding over,
giving a quarter turn and rolling out three
times, chilling for 20 minutes in between
each time. To make the filling, melt
4 tbsp butter and fry the shallots and garlic
until soft but not browned. Add the
remaining butter and the mushrooms and
cook for 35–40 minutes. Drain off any excess
liquid and stir in the remaining ingredients.
Let cool. Preheat the oven to 450°F.

4

Fold the outer two-thirds over, folding over
the uncovered third last. Seal the edges with
a rolling pin. Give the dough a quarter turn
and roll it out again. Mark it into thirds and
dot with the remaining butter cubes
in the same way.

6

Divide the pastry in two. Roll out one half
into a 9 in round, cutting around a plate to
make a neat shape. Pile the filling into the
center. Roll out the remaining pastry large
enough to cover the base. Brush the edges of
the base with water and then lay the second
pastry circle on top. Press the edges together
to seal and brush the top with a little beaten
egg. Bake for 45 minutes, or until the pastry
is risen, golden and flaky.

Mushroom and Parsley Soup

*Thickened with bread, this rich mushroom soup will warm you up
on cold autumn days. It makes a terrific hearty lunch.*

INGREDIENTS

*6 tbsp unsalted butter
2 lb mushrooms, trimmed, wiped
and sliced
2 onions, coarsely chopped
2½ cups milk
8 slices white bread
4 tbsp chopped fresh parsley
1¼ cups heavy cream
salt and freshly ground
black pepper*

Serves 8

1

Melt the butter and sauté the mushrooms
and onions until soft but not colored –
about 10 minutes. Add the milk.

2

Tear the bread into pieces, drop them into
the soup and let the bread soak for
15 minutes. Purée the soup and return it to
the pan. Add the parsley, cream and seasoning.
Reheat, but do not allow the soup to boil.
Serve at once.

Thyme-roasted Onions

*These slowly roasted onions develop a delicious sweet flavor which is delicious
with roast meat. You could prepare parboiled new potatoes in the same way.*

INGREDIENTS

*5 tbsp olive oil
4 tbsp unsalted butter
2 lb small onions
2 tbsp chopped fresh thyme
salt and freshly ground
black pepper*

Serves 4

1

Preheat the oven to 425°F. Heat the oil
and butter in a large roasting pan. Add
the onions and toss them in the oil and
butter mixture.

2

Add the thyme and seasoning and roast for
45 minutes, basting regularly.

Duck and Chestnut Casserole

Serve this casserole with a mixture of mashed potatoes and celeriac,
to soak up the rich duck juices.

INGREDIENTS

4½ lb duck
3 tbsp olive oil
6 oz small onions
2 oz field mushrooms
2 oz shiitake mushrooms
1¼ cups dry red wine
such as Cabernet Sauvignon
1¼ cups beef stock,
fresh or canned
8 oz canned, peeled,
unsweetened chestnuts, drained
salt and freshly ground
black pepper

Serves 4–6

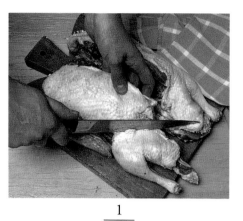

1

Cut the duck into eight pieces. Heat the oil
in a large frying pan and brown the duck
pieces. Remove from the frying pan.

2

Add the onions to the pan and brown them
well for 10 minutes.

3

Add the mushrooms and cook, stirring for
a few minutes more. Deglaze the pan with
the red wine and boil to reduce the
volume by half. Meanwhile, preheat the
oven to 350°F.

4

Pour the wine and the stock into a
casserole. Replace the duck, add the
chestnuts, season well and cook in the oven
for 1½ hours.

AUTUMN RECIPES

Cheese Scones

These delicious scones make a good tea-time or brunch treat. They are best served fresh and still slightly warm.

INGREDIENTS

2 cups all-purpose flour
2½ tsp baking powder
½ tsp mustard powder
½ tsp salt
4 tbsp butter, chilled and cubed
3 oz Cheddar cheese, grated
⅔ cup milk
1 egg, beaten

Makes 12

1

Preheat the oven to 450°F. Sift the flour, baking powder, mustard powder and salt into a mixing bowl. Add the butter and rub it into the flour mixture until the mixture resembles bread crumbs. Stir in 2 oz of the cheese.

2

Make a well in the center and add the milk and egg. Mix gently and then turn the dough out on to a lightly floured surface. Roll it out and cut it into triangles or squares. Brush lightly with milk and sprinkle with the remaining cheese. Let rest for 15 minutes, then bake them for 15 minutes, or until well risen.

Oatcakes

These are very simple to make and are an excellent addition to a cheese board.

INGREDIENTS

1⅔ cups oatmeal
¾ cup all-purpose flour
¼ tsp baking soda
tsp salt
2 tbsp Crisco
2 tbsp butter

Makes 24

1

Preheat the oven to 425°F. Place the oatmeal, flour, soda and salt in a large bowl. Gently melt the Crisco and butter together in a pan.

2

Add the melted fat and enough boiling water to make a soft dough. Turn out on to a surface scattered with a little oatmeal. Roll out the dough thinly and cut it into circles. Bake the oatcakes on ungreased baking sheets for 15 minutes, until crisp.

Blackberry Charlotte

A classic dessert, perfect for cold days. Serve with lightly whipped cream
or homemade custard.

INGREDIENTS

5 tbsp unsalted butter
3 cups fresh white bread crumbs
4 tbsp brown sugar
4 tbsp maple syrup
finely grated rind and juice
of 2 lemons
2 oz walnut halves
1 lb blackberries
1 lb cooking apples, peeled,
cored and finely sliced
whipped cream or
custard, to serve

Serves 4

1

Preheat the oven to 350°F. Grease a 2 cup
Pyrex dish with 1 tbsp of the butter. Melt the
remaining butter and add the bread crumbs.
Sauté them for 5–7 minutes, until the
crumbs are slightly crisp.and golden.
Leave to cool slightly.

2

Place the sugar, syrup, lemon rind and juice
in a small saucepan and gently warm them.
Add the crumbs.

3

Process the walnuts until they are
finely ground.

4

Arrange a thin layer of blackberries in the
dish. Top with a thin layer of crumbs.

5

Add a thin layer of apple, topping it with
another thin layer of crumbs. Repeat the
process with another layer of blackberries,
followed by a layer of crumbs. Continue
until you have used up all the ingredients,
finishing with a layer of crumbs.
The mixture should be piled well above
the top edge of the dish, because it shrinks
during cooking. Bake for 30 minutes, until
the crumbs are golden and the fruit is soft.

Poached Pears

Use a firm, sweet pear such as Bartlett or Anjou and serve warm.

INGREDIENTS

6 medium pears
1¾ cups superfine
sugar
3 tbsp honey
1 vanilla bean
2½ cups red wine
1 tsp whole cloves
3 in cinnamon stick
whipped cream to serve

Serves 4

1

Peel the pears but leave them whole,
keeping the stalks as well.

2

Put the sugar, honey, vanilla bean, wine,
cloves and cinnamon stick in a large pan.

3

Add the pears and poach until soft, about
30 minutes. When the pears are tender,
remove them with a slotted spoon and keep
them warm. Remove the vanilla bean, cloves
and cinnamon stick and boil the liquid
until it is reduced by half. Serve spooned
over the pears.

AUTUMN RECIPES

Steamed Ginger and Cinnamon Syrup Pudding

A traditional and comforting steamed pudding, best served with custard.

INGREDIENTS

9 tbsp softened butter
3 tbsp maple syrup
½ cup superfine sugar
2 eggs, lightly beaten
1 cup all-purpose flour
1 tsp baking powder
1 tsp ground cinnamon
1 oz preserved ginger,
finely chopped
2 tbsp milk
custard, to serve

Serves 4

___
1

Set a full steamer or saucepan of water on to boil. Lightly grease a 2½ cup pudding bowl with 1 tbsp butter. Place the maple syrup in the bowl.

___
2

Cream the remaining butter and sugar together until light and fluffy. Gradually add the eggs until the mixture is glossy. Sift the flour, baking powder and cinnamon together and fold them into the mixture, with the preserved ginger. Add the milk to make a soft, dropping consistency.

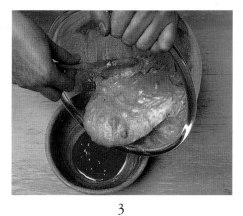

___
3

Spoon the batter into the bowl and smooth the top. Cover with a pleated piece of wax paper, to allow for expansion during cooking. Tie securely with string and steam for 1½–2 hours, making sure that the water level is kept topped up, to ensure a good flow of steam to cook the pudding. Turn the pudding out to serve it.

French Apple Tart

For added flavor, scatter some slivered almonds over the top of this classic tart.

INGREDIENTS

For the pastry
½ cup unsalted butter,
softened
4 tbsp vanilla sugar
1 egg
2 cups all-purpose flour

For the filling
4 tbsp unsalted butter
5 large tart apples, peeled, cored
and sliced
juice of ½ lemon
1¼ cups heavy cream
2 egg yolks
2 tbsp vanilla sugar
⅔ cup ground almonds,
toasted
2 tbsp slivered almonds, toasted,
to garnish

Serves 8

1

Place the butter and sugar in a food processor and process them well together. Add the egg —and process to mix it in well.

2

Add the flour and process till you have a soft dough. Wrap the dough in plastic wrap and chill it for 30 minutes.

3

Roll the pastry out on a lightly floured surface to about 9–10 in diameter.

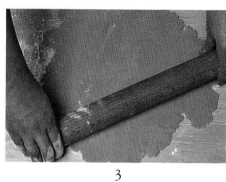

4

Line a pie pan with the pastry and chill it for a further 30 minutes. Preheat the oven to 425°F and place a baking sheet in the oven to heat up. Line the pastry case with wax paper and baking beans and bake blind on the baking sheet for 10 minutes. Then remove the beans and paper and cook for a further 5 minutes.

5

Turn the oven down to 375°F. To make the filling, melt the butter in a frying pan and lightly sauté the apples for 5–7 minutes. Sprinkle the apples with lemon juice.

6

Beat the cream and egg yolks with the sugar. Stir in the toasted ground almonds. Arrange the apple slices on top of the warm pastry and pour over the cream mixture. Bake for 25 minutes, or until the cream is just about set — it tastes better if the cream is still slightly runny in the center. Serve hot or cold, scattered with slivered almonds.

Winter Recipes

························

With the days growing shorter, we all need something substantial and warming to keep out the cold. Try roast beef with roasted peppers, or raised country pie. Scotch pancakes or cranberry muffins are a perfect fireside supper, and rich Christmas pudding is the perfect way to round off the year.

Roast Beef with Porcini and Sweet Bell Peppers

A substantial and warming dish for cold, dark evenings.

INGREDIENTS

3–3½ lb piece of sirloin
1 tbsp olive oil
1 lb small red bell peppers
4 oz mushrooms
6 oz thick-sliced pancetta
or bacon, cubed
2 tbsp all-purpose flour
⅔ cup full-bodied
red wine
1¼ cups beef stock
2 tbsp Marsala
2 tsp dried mixed herbs
salt and freshly ground
black pepper

Serves 8

1

Preheat the oven to 375°F. Season the meat well. Heat the olive oil in a large frying pan. When very hot, brown the meat on all sides. Place in a large roasting pan and cook for 1¼ hours.

2

Put the red peppers in the oven to roast for 20 minutes, if small ones are available, or 45 minutes if large ones are used.

3

Near the end of the meat's cooking time, prepare the gravy. Coarsely chop the mushroom caps and stems.

4

Heat the frying pan again and add the pancetta or bacon. Cook until the fat runs freely from the meat. Add the flour and cook for a few minutes until browned.

5

Gradually stir in the red wine and the stock. Bring to a boil, stirring. Lower the heat and add the Marsala, herbs and seasoning.

6

Add the mushrooms to the pan and heat through. Remove the sirloin from the oven and leave to stand for 10 minutes before carving it. Serve with the roasted peppers and the hot gravy.

WINTER RECIPES

Bacon and Lentil Soup

Serve this hearty soup with chunks of warm, crusty bread.

INGREDIENTS

*1 lb thick-sliced bacon,
cubed
1 onion, coarsely chopped
1 small turnip, coarsely chopped
1 celery stalk, chopped
1 carrot, sliced
1 potato, peeled and
coarsely chopped
½ cup lentils
1 bouquet garni
freshly ground black pepper*

Serves 4

1

Heat a large pan and add the bacon. Cook for
a few minutes, allowing the fat to run out.

2

Add all the vegetables and cook for
4 minutes.

3

Add the lentils, bouquet garni, seasoning
and enough water to cover. Bring to a boil
and simmer for 1 hour, or until the lentils
are tender.

Creamy Layered Potatoes

Cook the potatoes on top of the stove first to help the dish to bake more quickly.

INGREDIENTS

*3–3½ lb large potatoes, peeled
and sliced
2 large onions, sliced
6 tbsp unsalted butter
1¼ cups heavy cream
salt and freshly ground
black pepper*

Serves 6

1

Preheat the oven to 400°F. Blanch the sliced
potatoes for 2 minutes, and drain well.

2

Place the potatoes, onions, butter and cream
in a pan, stir well and cook for about
15 minutes. Transfer to a large ovenproof
dish, season well and bake for 1 hour, until
the potatoes are tender.

Traditional Beef Stew and Dumplings

This dish can cook in the oven while you go for a wintery walk to work up an appetite.

INGREDIENTS

1 tbsp all-purpose flour
2½ lb stewing beef,
cubed
2 tbsp olive oil
2 large onions, sliced
1 lb carrots, sliced
½ pint / 1¼ cups Guinness
or dark beer
3 bay leaves
2 tsp brown sugar
3 fresh thyme sprigs
1 tsp cider vinegar
salt and freshly ground
black pepper

For the dumplings
½ cup chopped Crisco
2 cups self-rising
flour
2 tbsp chopped mixed
fresh herbs
about ⅔ cup water

Serves 6

___1___

Preheat the oven to 325°F. Season the flour
and sprinkle over the meat, tossing to coat.

___2___

Heat the oil in a large casserole and lightly
sauté the onions and carrots. Remove the
vegetables with a slotted spoon and
reserve them.

___3___

Brown the meat well in batches
in the casserole.

___4___

Return all the vegetables to the casserole and
add any leftover seasoned flour. Add the
Guinness or beer, bay leaves, sugar and
thyme. Bring the liquid to a boil and then
transfer to the oven.

___6___

Form the dough into small balls with floured
hands. Add the cider vinegar to the meat and
spoon the dumplings on top. Cook for a
further 20 minutes, until the dumplings
have cooked through and serve hot.

___5___

After the meat has been cooking for 1 hour
and 40 minutes, make the dumplings. Mix
the Crisco and flour together. Add enough
water to make a soft, sticky dough.

Country Pie

*A classic raised pie. It takes quite a long time to make,
but is a perfect winter treat.*

1 small duck
1 small chicken
12 oz pork belly, minced
1 egg, lightly beaten
2 shallots, finely chopped
½ tsp ground cinnamon
½ tsp grated nutmeg
1 tsp Worcestershire sauce
finely grated rind of 1 lemon
½ tsp freshly ground black pepper
⅔ cup red wine
6 oz ham, cut into cubes
salt and freshly ground
black pepper

For the aspic
all the meat bones and trimmings
2 carrots
1 onion
2 celery stalks
1 tbsp red wine
1 bay leaf
1 whole clove
1 packet of gelatin
(about 1 oz)

For the pastry
1 cup Crisco
1¼ cups boiling water
6 cups all-purpose flour
1 egg, lightly beaten with a
pinch of salt

Serves 12

1

Cut as much meat from the raw duck and chicken as possible, removing the skin and sinews. Cut the duck and chicken breasts into cubes and set them aside.

2

Mix the rest of the duck and chicken meat with the minced pork, egg, shallots, spices, Worcestershire sauce, lemon rind and salt and pepper. Add the red wine and leave for about 15 minutes for the flavors to develop.

3

To make the aspic, place the meat bones and trimmings, carrots, onion, celery, wine, bay leaf and clove in a large pan and cover with 12½ cups of water. Bring to a boil, skimming off any scum, and simmer gently for 2½ hours.

4

To make the pastry, place the fat and water in a pan and bring to a boil. Sift the flour with a pinch of salt into a bowl and pour on the hot liquid. Mix with a wooden spoon, and, when the dough is cool enough to handle, knead it well and let it sit in a warm place, covered with a cloth, for 20–30 minutes or until you are ready to use it. Preheat the oven to 400°F.

5

Grease a 10 in loose-based deep cake pan. Roll out about two-thirds of the pastry thinly enough to line the cake pan. Make sure there are no holes and allow enough pastry to leave a little hanging over the top. Fill the pie with a layer of half the minced-pork mixture; then top this with a layer of the cubed duck and chicken breast-meat and cubes of ham. Top with the remaining minced pork. Brush the overhanging edges of pastry with water and cover with the remaining rolled-out pastry. Seal the edges well. Make two large holes in the top and decorate with any pastry trimmings.

6

Bake the pie for 30 minutes. Brush the top with the egg and salt mixture. Turn down the oven to 350°F. After 30 minutes loosely cover the pie with foil to prevent the top getting too brown, and bake it for a further 1 hour.

7

Strain the stock after 2½ hours. Let it cool and remove the solidified layer of fat from the surface. Measure 2½ cups of stock. Heat it gently to just below boiling point and whisk the gelatin into it until no lumps are left. Add the remaining strained stock and leave to cool.

8

When the pie is cool, place a funnel through one of the holes and pour in as much of the stock as possible, letting it come up to the holes in the crust. Leave to set for at least 24 hours before slicing and serving.

Leek and Onion Tart

This unusual recipe isn't a normal tart with pastry, but an all-in-one savory slice that is excellent served as an accompaniment to roast meat.

INGREDIENTS

4 tbsp unsalted butter
12 oz leeks, sliced thinly
2 cups self-rising flour
1/2 cup Crisco
2/3 cup water
salt and freshly ground
black pepper

Serves 4

1

Preheat the oven to 400°F. Melt the butter in a pan and sauté the leeks until soft. Season well.

2

Mix the flour, fat and water together in a bowl to make a soft but sticky dough. Mix into the leek mixture in the pan. Place in a greased shallow ovenproof dish and bake for 30 minutes, or until brown and crispy. Serve sliced, as a vegetable accompaniment.

Orange Shortbread Fingers

These are a real tea-time treat. The fingers will keep in an airtight tin for up to two weeks.

INGREDIENTS

½ cup unsalted butter,
softened
4 tbsp superfine sugar,
plus a little extra
finely grated rind of 2 oranges
1½ cups all-purpose flour

Makes 18

1

Preheat the oven to 375°F. Beat the butter and sugar together until they are soft and creamy. Beat in the orange rind.

2

Gradually add the flour and gently pull the dough together to form a soft ball. Roll the dough out on a lightly floured surface until about ½ in thick. Cut it into fingers, sprinkle over a little extra superfine sugar, prick with a fork and bake for about 20 minutes, or until the fingers are a light golden color.

Cranberry Muffins

A tea or breakfast dish that is not too sweet.

INGREDIENTS

3 cups all-purpose flour
1 tsp baking powder
pinch of salt
½ cup superfine sugar
2 eggs
⅔ cup milk
4 tbsp corn oil
finely grated rind of 1 orange
5 oz cranberries

Makes 12

1

Preheat the oven to 375°F. Line a muffin pan with paper cases. Mix the flour, baking powder, salt and superfine sugar together.

2

Lightly beat the eggs with the milk and oil. Add them to the dry ingredients and blend to make a smooth batter. Stir in the orange rind and cranberries. Divide the mixture between the muffin cases and bake for 25 minutes until risen and golden. Let cool in the pan for a few minutes, and serve warm or cold.

Country Pancakes

Serve these hot with butter and maple syrup or jam.

INGREDIENTS

2 cups self-rising flour
4 tbsp superfine sugar
4 tbsp butter, melted
1 egg
1¼ cups milk
1 tbsp corn oil or margarine

Makes 24

1

Mix the flour and sugar together. Add the melted butter and egg with two-thirds of the milk. Mix to a smooth batter – it should be thin enough to find its own level.

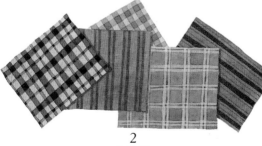

2

Heat a griddle or a heavy-based frying pan and wipe it with a little oil or margarine. When hot, drop spoonfuls of the mixture on to the hot griddle or pan. When bubbles come to the surface of the pancakes, flip them over to cook until golden on the other side. Keep the pancakes warm wrapped in a dish towel while cooking the rest of the mixture. Serve as soon as possible.

Christmas Pudding

The classic Christmas dessert. Wrap it in cheesecloth and store it in an airtight container for up to a year for the flavors to develop.

INGREDIENTS

1 cup all-purpose flour
pinch of salt
1 tsp ground allspice
½ tsp ground cinnamon
¼ tsp freshly grated nutmeg
1 cup grated hard Crisco
1 apple, grated
2 cups fresh white
bread crumbs
1⅞ cups soft brown
sugar
2 oz slivered almonds
1½ cups seedless raisins
1½ cups currants
1½ cups golden raisins
4 oz ready-to-eat dried
apricots
¾ cup chopped mixed
citrus peel
finely grated rind and juice
of 1 lemon
2 tbsp molasses
3 eggs
1¼ cups milk
2 tbsp rum

Serves 8

<u>1</u>

Sift the flour, salt and spices into
a large bowl.

<u>2</u>

Add the Crisco, apple and other dry
ingredients, including the grated
lemon rind.

<u>3</u>

Heat the molasses until warm and runny
and pour into the dry ingredients.

<u>4</u>

Mix together the eggs, milk, rum
and lemon juice.

<u>5</u>

Stir the liquid into the dry mixture.

<u>6</u>

Spoon the mixture into two 5 cup bowls.
Wrap the puddings with pieces of wax paper,
pleated to allow for expansion, and tie with
string. Steam the puddings in a steamer or
saucepan of boiling water. Each pudding
needs 10 hours' cooking and 3 hours'
reheating. Remember to keep the water level
topped up to keep the pans from boiling dry.
Serve decorated with holly.

Gifts from the Pantry

....

*Make the most of seasonal fruits and vegetables,
by making jams, jellies and preserves to enjoy
the year round, or to give as gifts.
Country favorites include strawberry jam,
apple and mint jelly, or piccalilli.*

Apple and Mint Jelly

This jelly is delicious served with garden peas, as well as the more traditional rich roasted meat such as lamb.

INGREDIENTS

2 lb cooking apples
granulated sugar
3 tbsp chopped fresh mint

Makes 3 × 1 lb jars

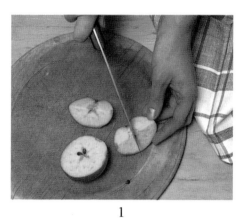

1

Chop the apples coarsely and put them in a preserving pan.

2

Add enough water to cover. Simmer until the fruit is soft.

3

Pour through a jelly bag, allowing it to drip overnight. Do not squeeze the bag or the jelly will become cloudy.

4

Measure the amount of juice. To every 2½ cups of juice, add 2¾ cups granulated sugar.

5

Place the juice and sugar in a large pan and heat gently. Dissolve the sugar and then bring to a boil. Test for setting, by pouring about 1 tbsp into a saucer and leaving to cool slightly. If a wrinkle forms on the surface when pushed with a fingertip, the jelly will set. When a set is reached, leave to cool.

6

Stir in the mint and pour into sterilized jars. Seal each jar with a waxed disc and a tightly fitting plastic top. Store in a cool, dark place. The jelly will keep unopened for up to a year. Once opened, keep in the fridge and consume within a week.

Lemon and Lime Curd

*Serve this creamy, tangy spread with toast or muffins,
instead of jam, for a delightful change.*

INGREDIENTS

½ cup unsalted butter   grated rind and juice of 2 lemons

3 eggs   grated rind and juice of 2 limes

1⅛ cups superfine sugar

Makes 2 × 1 lb jars

1

Set a heatproof mixing bowl over a large pan
of simmering water. Add the butter.

2

Lightly beat the eggs and add them
to the butter.

3

Add the lemon and lime rinds and juices,
then add the sugar.

4

Stir the mixture constantly until it thickens.
Pour into sterilized jars. Seal each jar with a
waxed disc and a tightly fitting plastic top.
Store in a cool, dark place. The curd will
keep unopened for up to a month.
Once opened, keep in the fridge and
consume within a week.

Poached Spiced Plums in Brandy

Canning spiced fruit is a great way to preserve summer flavors for eating in winter. Serve these with whipped cream as a dessert.

INGREDIENTS

2½ cups brandy
rind of 1 lemon, peeled in a
long strip
1⅔ cups superfine sugar
1 cinnamon stick
2 lb fresh plums

Makes 2 lb

1

Put the brandy, lemon rind, sugar and cinnamon stick in a large pan and heat gently to dissolve the sugar. Add the plums and poach for 15 minutes, or until soft. Remove with a slotted spoon.

2

Reduce the syrup by a third by rapid boiling. Strain it over the plums. Pack the plums in large sterilized jars. Seal tightly and store for up to 6 months in a cool, dark place.

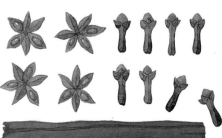

Spiced Pickled Pears

*These delicious pears are the perfect accompaniment for cooked ham
or cold meat salads.*

INGREDIENTS

2 lb pears
2½ cups white-wine
vinegar
1⅛ cups superfine sugar
1 cinnamon stick
5 star anise
10 whole cloves

Makes 2 lb

1

Peel the pears, keeping them whole
and leaving on the stalks. Heat the vinegar
and sugar together until the sugar has melted.
Pour over the pears and poach for 15 minutes.

2

Add the cinnamon, star anise and cloves
and simmer for 10 minutes. Remove the
pears and pack tightly into sterilized jars.
Simmer the syrup for a further 15 minutes
and pour it over the pears. Seal the jars
tightly and store in a cool, dark place. The
pears will keep for up to a year unopened.
Once opened, store in the fridge and
consume within a week.

Tomato Chutney

*This spicy chutney is delicious with a selection of cheeses and biscuits,
or with cold meats.*

INGREDIENTS

2 lb tomatoes, skinned 1 ⅛ cups superfine sugar
1 ⅓ cups raisins 2 ½ cups cider
8 oz onions, chopped vinegar

Makes 4 × 1 lb jars

1

Chop the tomatoes coarsely. Put them in
a preserving pan.

2

Add the raisins, onions and sugar.

3

Pour over the vinegar. Bring to a boil
and let it simmer for 2 hours, uncovered.
Pot into sterilized jars. Seal with a waxed disc
and cover with a tightly fitting plastic
top. Store in a cool, dark place. The chutney
will keep unopened for up to a year. Once
opened, store in the fridge and consume
within a week.

Strawberry Jam

This classic recipe is always popular. Make sure the jam is allowed to cool before pouring into jars so the fruit doesn't float to the top.

INGREDIENTS

*3–3 ½ lb strawberries
juice of ½ lemon
3–3 ½ lb granulated sugar*

Makes about 5 lb

1

Hull the strawberries.

2

Put the strawberries in a pan with the lemon juice. Mash a few of the strawberries. Let the fruit simmer for 20 minutes or until softened.

3

Add the sugar and let it dissolve slowly over a gentle heat. Then let the jam boil rapidly until a setting point is reached.

4

Let stand until the strawberries are well distributed through the jam. Pack into sterilized jars. Seal each jar with a waxed disc and cover with a tightly fitting plastic top. Store in a cool dark place. The jam may be kept unopened for up to a year. Once opened, keep in the fridge and consume within a week.

Three-fruit Marmalade

Homemade marmalade may be time-consuming but the results are incomparably better than storebought varieties.

INGREDIENTS

12 oz oranges
12 oz lemons
1½ lb grapefruit
10¼ cups water
6 lb granulated sugar

Makes 6 × 1 lb jars

1

Rinse the fruit and dry them.

2

Put the fruit in a preserving pan. Add the water and let it simmer for about 2 hours.

3

Quarter the fruit, remove the pulp and add it to the pan with the cooking liquid.

4

Cut the rinds into slivers, and add to the pan. Add the sugar. Gently heat until the sugar has dissolved. Bring to a boil and cook until a setting point is reached. Let stand for 1 hour to allow the peel to settle. Pour into sterilized jars. Seal each jar with a waxed disc and a tightly fitting plastic top. Store in a cool, dark place.

GIFTS FROM THE PANTRY

Piccalilli

The piquancy of this relish partners well with sausages, bacon or ham.

INGREDIENTS

1½ lb cauliflower   1 tsp dry mustard powder
1 lb small onions   2 tsp corn starch
12 oz green beans   2½ cups vinegar
1 tsp ground turmeric

Makes 3 × 1 lb jars

1

Cut the cauliflower into tiny florets.

2

Peel the onions and top and tail
the green beans.

3

In a small saucepan, measure in the turmeric,
mustard powder and corn starch, and pour
over the vinegar. Stir well and simmer
for 10 minutes.

4

Pour the vinegar mixture over the vegetables
in a pan, mix well and simmer
for 45 minutes.

5

Pour into sterilized jars. Seal each jar with a
waxed disc and a tightly fitting plastic
top. Store in a cool dark place. The piccalilli
will keep unopened for up to a year. Once
opened store in the fridge and consume
within a week.

Rosemary-flavored Oil

This pungent oil is ideal drizzled over meat or vegetables before grilling.

INGREDIENTS

2½ cups olive oil
5 fresh rosemary sprigs

Makes 2½ cups

1

Heat the oil until warm but not too hot.

2

Add four rosemary sprigs and heat gently.
Put the reserved rosemary sprig in a clean
bottle. Strain the oil, pour in the bottle and
seal tightly. Allow to cool and store in a
cool, dark place. Use within a week.

Thyme-flavored Vinegar

This vinegar is delicious sprinkled over salmon intended for poaching.

INGREDIENTS

2½ cups white-wine
vinegar
5 fresh thyme sprigs
3 garlic cloves, peeled

Makes 2½ cups

1

Warm the vinegar.

2

Add four thyme sprigs and the garlic and
heat gently. Put the reserved thyme sprig in
a clean bottle, strain the vinegar, and add to
the bottle. Seal tightly, allow to cool and
store in a cool, dark place. The vinegar
may be kept unopened for up to 3 months.

Index

Acknowledgements

Tessa Evelegh would like to thank Lindsay Porter for all her inspiration and encouragement in putting this book together, *Practical Gardening* magazine for all their support, Michelle Garrett for her wonderful, vibrant photographs and James and Madeleine for their encouragement and friendship.

Tessa and the publishers would also like to thank Fiona Barnett at Manic Botanic for the wheat heart on page 120, Eileen Simpson at Hill Farm Herbs for supplying the dried-herb wreath on page 136 and Somerset House of Iron for the chair featured on the jacket.

Suppliers

Adventures in Crafts
Yorkville Station
P.O. Box 6058
New York, NY 10128
(212) 410-97935
(Découpage products, wood products, gilding supplies, moldable epoxy and other adhesives, sizing and mini-tool kits.)

Bear Woods Supply Co.
P.O. Box 40
Bear River, Nova Scotia BOS 1B0 Canada
(902) 467-3703
(Unfinished wood ware, including candle cups, holders, sticks, Shaker pegs, other pegs, wheels, toys, kitchen items, spindles, finials, dowels and more.

Homestead Handicrafts
1301 N. Pines Road
Spokane, WA 99206
(509) 928-1986
(Tôle decorative painting supplies, including paints, brushes and cleaners, canvas, mediums, stencils, resins, stains, finishes and unfinished wood.)

Stubbs Old Village Paints/Old Sturbridge Paints
P.O. Box 597
East Allen and Graham Streets
Allentown, PA 18105
(Reproduction and natural pigment paints)

Tom Thumb Workshops
P.O. Box 357
Mappsville, VT 23407
(804) 824-3507
(Natural supplies: dried flowers, cones and pods, containers and supplies: ribbons, floral items, moss, silica, foam. Also offers wire, straw and moss wreaths, a full line of spices, herbs and essential oils.)